MEXICAN LANDSCAPE ARCHITECTURE

FROM THE STREET AND FROM WITHIN

ROSINA GREENE KIRBY

THE UNIVERSITY OF ARIZONA PRESS

TUCSON, ARIZONA

About the Author.....

ROSINA GREENE KIRBY spent her childhood in Mexico, absorbing the aesthetics of the environment, developing a profound interest in the people, and becoming fluent in the Spanish language that helped to make this book possible. She was an art student at the Instituto de Bellas Artes in Mexico City, and graduated cum laude in art from the University of Arizona where in 1971 she earned also a master's degree in landscape architecture, in which field she is a professional consultant. An Arizonan since the 1950's she also teaches in Tucson. She has made many extended trips to Mexico for researching and in some instances personally photographing dramatic sites presented in this volume. In 1972, Mrs. Kirby was named in *Outstanding Young Women of America*.

Unless otherwise credited, photographs for this volume were taken by the author, Rosina G. Kirby.

THE UNIVERSITY OF ARIZONA PRESS

Copyright © November 1972
The Arizona Board of Regents
All Rights Reserved
Manufactured in the U.S.A.

I. S. B. N.-0-8165-0327-3
L. C. No. 72-83818

TO THE FIVE

CONTENTS

Indexed List of Illustrations

AUTHOR'S NOTE

MORE THAN SIX HUNDRED YEARS of Mexican environmental design provided the various influences and determinants which have brought about the Mexican landscape as it appears today. To incorporate all examples from any given period of Mexican landscape architecture is an impossibility; the individual sites depicted and discussed in the book serve as keystones, representing the various facets which make up the whole.

In the chapters on contemporary landscape architecture, the book focuses at length on the work of one man, Luis Barragán. It is largely through his efforts that landscape architecture in Mexico has emerged as a profession in its own right. Trained as an architect and engineer, he nonetheless has directed his efforts to dealing with the landscape as a separate and specialized entity. In this context he is to landscape architecture what José Villagrán García was to Mexican architecture in the 1930s—a catalyst breathing life into an environmental art form endangered by stagnation and repetition. The solutions of the past served the needs of a definite era; today's problems cannot be solved by the methods of yesterday. Barragán's work embodies this premise.

In any civilization, the intrinsic values and convictions which are inherent in that society dictate the form and direction of its man-made environment. Throughout centuries, this basic element has been vividly present in the Mexican landscape—a tangible interaction between the Mexican state of mind and the visible quality of the landscape. This is the crux of landscape architecture—the kinetic communion between man, earth, and space.

Nowhere was this relationship more evident than in the Aztec capital of Tenochtitlán. The Aztecs—a mystic, fierce, spartan people—fanatically embraced a faith which governed their every action, extending even to the design of their physical surroundings. The consummate bond between these people, their religion, and the treatment of their landscape is recorded in their codices. The extent to which the Aztec code of laws relates to the layout of their capital is by no means negligible. Archaeologists, historians, and anthropologists throughout the years have translated, interpreted, and disseminated this ancient legacy. In the text that follows, the essence of certain of these codices is conveyed in poetic form, rather than dwelling at length in conventional prose.

ACKNOWLEDGMENTS

A book of this nature can come about only through the collaboration of many people. Although thousands of miles separate these friends and colleagues, their common interest and good will knew no boundaries and have irrevocably bound them through this common effort.

My heartfelt thanks go to the University of Arizona Alumni Association, the Sunbonnet Garden Club of Tucson, Arizona, the University of Arizona Foundation, and most

Photograph by Armando Salas Portugal

13

especially to Mr. and Mrs. John W. Murphey, all of whom assisted in funding this work through various stages of its development to its final presentation.

The help and patience of the Instituto Nacional de Antropología e Historia was invaluable, notably in the personages of Ignacio Bernal and Ignacio Marquina of the Museum of Anthropology, and Lic. Mariano Monterrosa Prado and his staff of archivists at Culhuacán.

Equally generous and gracious was the staff of *Artes de México*, headed by Sr. Don José Losada Tomé, whose advice and assistance never faltered. I am grateful to the National Geographic Society and to Clive B. Smith, author of *Builders in the Sun*, for their cooperation and contribution of several key photographs.

My appreciation goes also to the staff of the University of Arizona Press, who approached the presentation, design, and publication of this work in a totally sensitive and sympathetic manner.

The work would not have begun had it not been for the encouragement of Professor Guy S. Greene, head of the School of Landscape Architecture at the University of Arizona. I am grateful for his "Word to the Reader" at the beginning of the book which serves as a frame of reference for the work that follows. His support and that of his colleague, Professor Warren D. Jones, transcend formal acknowledgment.

ROSINA G. KIRBY

A WORD TO THE READER

LANDSCAPE ARCHITECTURE as a distinct and separate profession is a fairly recent phenomenon, although its roots and traditions are as old as civilization. Wherever men have settled they have created a structured environment which, in many societies, has been done as a thoughtful and deliberate art.

One of the most important aspects of any work in environmental design is the development of a sense of place and identity. It is this quality which is such a significant part of landscape design in Mexico. Design in Mexico is Mexican design, not only in the evident features involving color, texture, and form, but also in the intangible qualities of scale, proportion, and spatial relationships. These represent a direct response to the hierarchy of values of the Mexican people themselves; here is still a country that can place aesthetic values above physical comfort.

This book, in exploring the intimate relationships between society and environment in Mexico, traces the highlights of this people and their land from the beginnings of Prehispanic history to the present. It is significant that the garden villas of the Aztec emperors, rulers of a people whom many consider neolithic, coincide in time and concept with those created during the Italian Renaissance.

As important an impact as was Prehispanic environmental design, any attempt to trace influences can be dangerous. One can perhaps discern in the work of contemporary designers the strength and dynamism of their Prehispanic heritage. It would probably be more accurate to say that their work represents the product of original, creative minds, responding in their own way to the interaction of natural and human events.

The major function of landscape design is the establishment of a harmonious relationship between man and nature. In the treatment of outdoor space for human use, Mexico has — throughout her history — exhibited an extraordinary feeling and sensitivity rarely found elsewhere. This is evident in the magnificent relations between volumes and spaces of pre-Cortesian sites, persisting even during the time of Spanish domination and periods of European eclecticism. Spanish patios were never quite Spanish but Mexican; plazas were not medieval town squares but distinctly Mexican.

The environment providing the physical setting for most human activity is the city, and its design is a difficult and complex process. As cities have grown in size and complexity, the use of land itself, heretofore always plentiful, has become a matter of critical concern. The landscape architect today directs his attention to this vast aspect of the environment — the use and development of land. He is concerned with the design of the individual private garden, the public garden or park, the character of streets and highways, the use and preservation of natural landscape reservations, and ultimately, the broad policies and techniques of land planning on a regional and national scale.

In the years ahead, we face a man-made environment from which there is no escape. In building such an environment, man inevitably reflects many of his attitudes about himself, the world, and his relation to nature. In turn, the environment shapes man.

In this enterprise examination of the historical development of our present civilization remains one of our most valuable tools. In the United States, we have been so preoccupied with the influence derived from western Europe and to some extent, the Orient, that we have tended to ignore Mexico's remarkable contributions to this field. Literature has been sadly deficient in examining this most vital, vigorous, and important contributor to the profession. We liberally use the terms, patio and plaza—yet what has been written of their roots? We discuss at great length the importance of New York's Central Park, which was, after all, directly derived from similar parks in England. Mexico's first park, Chapultepec, was designed in 1440 and dedicated to the public in 1530—more than three hundred years earlier.

In the last few decades, Mexico's sense of its own identity has increased manifold. Its contemporary designers are imaginative, daring, and original without losing innate sensitivity in the use of materials, form, and space, nor the response to nature which expresses the Mexican character. It is the essence of this character to which we now turn—one which will add its own dimension to the field and one from which we can learn much.

ONE

THE VIEW
FROM THE STREET

Painting by Ignacio Marquina, *courtesy Instituto Nacional de Antropología e Historia.*

TEMPLE PRECINCT OF TENOCHTITLÁN.

The glimmer of water consumes the eye
      its reflection of infinite planes
Shattered by the wake of unconcerned canoes.
There is a venous odor
      overlaid with that of marigold.

Tenochtitlán
      lake place high on the plateau
Surrounded by mountains, volcanic barriers,
      trapping the rainwater
            forbidding its runoff
                  creating the lakes:
My city
      an indigenous gem embraced by a basaltic crown.
Tenochtitlán

16TH CENTURY MAP OF TENOCHTITLÁN.
From the original plan attributed to Cortés.

THE PREHISPANIC HERITAGE

THE VALLEY OF MEXICO, originally called Anáhuac (*Near the Water*) nestles within a ring of volcanic mountains in the central plateau of Mexico, 7244 feet above sea level. A series of shallow lakes, made brackish by the lack of drainage, originally covered the basin floor. From an island near the southwest shore of one of these lakes, the lake of Texcoco, sprang the Aztec civilization whose achievements in environmental design were the epitome of Prehispanic cultures.

There is no doubt that the incredible artistry of the Aztec civilization was the product of more than two thousand years of preceding Mesoamerican cultures; cultures whose proficiency in the environmental arts served as exemplary models culminating in the spectacular capital of Tenochtitlán. In ghostly succession, each culture as it developed and died left its possible contribution for the Aztecs, who in turn adapted and incorporated the essence of each into their own civilization.

Among these was the Olmec, 2000 B.C., labeled the Mother Culture by Covarrubias. Its sculptors were masters of stone and jade. Their gargantuan carved heads, sensuous and feline, demonstrated an affinity with stone which set forth a legacy of incomparable value for subsequent civilizations.

On the highlands of Oaxaca the Zapotecs produced Monte Albán, whose core was the Great Plaza, hailed as being one of the most beautiful open spaces ever conceived by man.

The roll of ancient masters goes on—Mixtec, Totonec, Maya. In landscape architecture, however, the most influential and notable contributor—not for gardens, for no trace or records remain, but for regional site design—was Teotihuacán.

Established in 200 B.C., Teotihuacán was the first fully developed urban center of Mesoamerica. This was a city whose concepts and implementation of land use serve as the greatest example of Precolumbian site planning. For the first time, a large permanent population was incorporated whose density has not been equaled by any previous culture in America. Its components were a ruling beaurocracy and distinctly separate social classes.

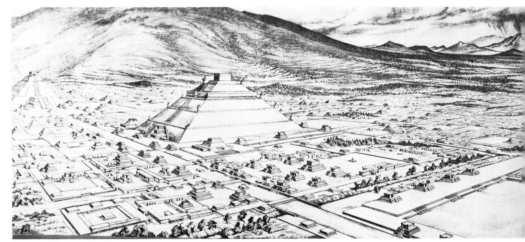

TEOTIHUACÁN. *Courtesy I.N.A.H.*

Cradled between two parallel mountain ranges, the general layout of Teotihuacán was cruciform, based on square modules. Its ceremonial center, the majestic Street of the Dead, followed a main longitudinal north-south axis. This great avenue stretched from the Pyramid of the Moon on its northern extreme to the sunken square of the Citadel, almost four miles away. The site of the Citadel surrounded the beautifully detailed temple of Quetzalcoatl, enriched by awesome stone heads of plumed serpents, symbol of the god Quetzalcoatl, alternating with other divinities.

Since the San Juan river intersects the Street of the Dead, the change of elevation is considerable. The designers of Teotihuacán overcame this problem

Courtesy I.N.A.H.

PYRAMID OF THE SUN, TEOTIHUACÁN.

by providing stepped terraces, which not only solved the dilemma but also removed any possibility of monotony which might have been induced by a level stretch of this size.

The temples and palaces flanking the sides of the Street of the Dead were dominated by the monumentally proportioned Pyramid of the Sun. A staggering structure, its base measures approximately 700 feet square and its height at the original summit was 200 feet. Surprisingly, the Pyramid of the Sun faces the processional avenue from its eastern flank, an asymmetric placement which departs from the symmetry characteristic of Teotihuacán. Another puzzling feature, considering the importance of the pyramid, is that it lacks access from its principal western facade to the Street of the Dead.

The sobriety of the open spaces of Teotihuacán is defined by its massive structures, austere and uninterrupted by semi-open buildings or colonnades, consciously and distinctly echoing the shape and character of the surrounding valleys and mountains. Here is a study of elegant balance between natural and man-made masses and voids, a rational harmony between natural topography and human environment, a site whose quality is suspended in time and place. Dr. Ignacio Bernal director of the Museum of Anthropology, in his *Mexico Before Cortés*, best describes the eternal quality of Teotihuacán,

Today, after a thousand years of abandonment and pillage, the sacred city is still magnificent and imposing in the austerity of its wisely open spaces combined with the majesty of the pyramids. Here everything was done to elevate the soul of the onlooker. It was not a matter of pleasing but of exalting.

Detail, temple of Quetzalcoatl, Teotihuacán.

As in most instances, the character of the urban landscape strongly reveals the nature of its people. Ruled by gods and priests, Teotihuacán was a peaceful, theocratic civilization, its faith manifested in the splendid serenity of its linear ceremonial complex; a people whose stability and orderliness were demonstrated by the rhythmical organization and arrangement of their streets and courtyards. Unfortified and open, the city reflected a society which was unoppressed and secure. Tragically, it was this latter quality which resulted in its destruction. Toward the second half of the ninth century, the city fell prey to nomadic bandits. Undefended and vulnerable, Teotihuacán was sacked and burned, a victim of its own boundless design.

Nearly two hundred years after the death of Teotihuacán the extraordinary Toltecs swept down from the north to establish the first of the militaristic empires which augured the total imperialism of the Aztec empire nearly five centuries later. In A.D. 980 the Toltecs founded their legendary capital of Tula, less than 100 miles northwest of the charred remains of Teotihuacán. The militaristic nature of these people is evident in the spartan aspect of the main square of the capital. This quadrangular area, 120 yards on each side, was closed on the north by an elevated stone colonnade behind which loomed the main pyramid. From the top of the pyramid a phalanx of immense stone warriors pierced the sky. Like colossal sentinels guarding the square, these warriors, fully armed with knives and breastplates, commanded the panorama of Tula.

Colossal warriors of stone were built in segments and placed on top of the pyramids without beasts of burden or the use of wheels. The construction of pre-Hispanic capitals, with their monumental pyramids and ceremonial temples, entailed a labor force equal to that used in the building of Imperial Rome.

TULA.

Painting courtesy of I.N.A.H.

Courtesy National Geographic Society: Photograph by W.E. Garrett

GREAT PYRAMID OF TULA.
Courtesy I.N.A.H.

Fifteen-foot high warriors bristle from the summit of the Great Pyramid of Tula. The stoic-faced Atlantes symbolized the Toltecs' militaristic prowess, which between the eighth and ninth centuries led them to establish the first warrior empire of the Americas.

25

The elegant simplicity and serenity of Teotihuacán contrast sharply with the richness of the Toltec style, which revels in a brilliant usage of bas-relief abstract forms and realistic representations of animals and warriors. The landscape architectural significance of Tula lies in the disposition of the structures and open spaces of its main square. The quadrangular design of this ceremonial center provided a transition between the linear layout of Teotihuacán and the cluster type later developed by the Aztecs in Tenochtitlán. The influence of Toltec artistry continued even after the political decline of Tula in the twelfth century. The prestige of its environmental art persisted and served to a great extent as a basis for the Aztecs who followed a century later.

The Aztecs first arrived in the Valley of Anáhuac in the early thirteenth century, a mystic, aggressive people who had wandered south from their legendary home of Aztlán. Weak and powerless, the newcomers hovered on the edge of Lake Texcoco, subject to the whims and dictates of their powerful neighbors. Native chroniclers relate how the Tepanec ruler of nearby Atzcapotzalco, one of these previously established tribes, demanded the yearly tribute of a floating raft garden planted with flowers and juniper trees for the landscaping of his capital. Not only were the plants to be in perfect condition, but the outlandish request also included a duck and a heron which were to hatch their eggs on the moment of arrival. For more than a hundred years the miserable Aztecs paid their tribute, served as mercenaries and waited patiently for a sign from their god Huitzilopochtli to establish a site for their permanent home.

In 1325 the momentous event took place. Huitzilopochtli's command was heard by two priests:

> *Hear me, for there is something that you have not seen. Go at once to see the Tenoch, on which you will see an eagle happily resting, sunning himself there, and you should be pleased, for this is where the heart of Copil was born. We shall find ourselves equipped with arrow and shield, and conquer and sieze all those who surround us for here will be our Mexican homelend, the place where the eagle screams and spreads his wings and eats, the place where the serpent is torn apart and many things will happen.*

The priests obeyed, went to the appointed place and beheld a rock protruding from the lake. Out of a crevice grew a prickly pear cactus, bearing the weight of an eagle devouring a serpent. On this site, surrounded by the lake, the Aztecs began to build their city, Tenochtitlán. By driving cane stakes into the bottom of the shallow lake and weaving reeds between them, the Aztecs created a wattled enclosure which was then filled by layers of sod and mud dredged from the lake bottom. These mud islands, chinampas, served as foundations for the homes and temples, as well as seed beds for the cultivation of vegetables

MIXQUIC, D. F.

Similar to the chinampas of Tenochtitlán, Mixquic is one of the last remaining examples of the man-made islands. The water hyacinth in the foreground is not native but was introduced to Mexico after the Conquest. It has since become a nuisance, choking the canals and preventing passage by canoe.

Photograph by Armando Salas Portugal

and flowers. Willows were also planted so that their roots would intertwine, anchoring the chinampa to the bottom of the lake. The chinampas, often mistakenly referred to as "floating" islands, became with the passage of time an integral part of the lake bottom by the strong network of the willows' root system. Each year, after the rainy season, the resulting erosion was counteracted by refilling and eventually enlarging the chinampas with rich, dredged soil. The city was originally made up of two principal chinampas separated by a dredged canal. One of these eventually became the site of the main market place of Tlatelolco; the other grew into the religious temple precinct of Tenochtitlán. As the power and population of the Aztecs increased, the chinampas grew in number and in size, eventually sustaining a city of 80,000 inhabitants and covering an area of five square miles, a figure exceeded at the time only by Milan, Rome, and Paris. The selection of this watery site for the establishment of a capital city appears to be, at best, bizarre. The fabrication of the chinampas alone seems to have been an impossible chore. It proved, however, to be a brilliant choice. Strategically and politically the site was invulnerable; its defense was remarkably simple since it could be attacked only by water. Situated in the center of hostile kingdoms, it owed allegiance to none.

By the middle of the fifteenth century the Aztecs had managed to overthrow all vestiges of bondage and had in turn subjugated their enemies or allied themselves with their less hostile neighbors. A hierarchy was established which, by the time of the Spanish Conquest in 1521, had produced a dynasty of six generations. Of these monarchs, three emerge as major contributors to the urban development of Tenochtitlán: Itzcóatl, Moctezuma I, and Moctezuma II. Netzahualcoyotl, ruler of the allied kingdom of Texcoco across the lake, also contributed much in this field. A remarkable man, Netzahualcoyotl was poet, philosopher, lawgiver and naturalist, emerging as the Mexican counterpart of the Renaissance Man of fifteenth-century Italy.

Itzcóatl, 1427-1440, the first of the landplanners and fourth ruler of this dynasty, is credited with having established the basically cruciform plan of Tenochtitlán. It was under his rule that the Aztecs began the building of the broad, straight causeways which linked the city to the mainland: the causeway of Tepeyac to the northern shore of the lake; Tlacopan to the west; and Iztapalapa to the south. The causeway on the eastern end of Tenochtitlán ended in a quay for the unloading of cargo by canoes. The design of these main causeways, pointing as they did to the four cardinal directions, was steeped with religious significance, Aztec society being totally theocratic.

QUETZALCOATL.
Codex Borbonicus, adapted from Miguel Covarrubias' painting.

North: *Black zenith of moon sky*
      Heaven of male night-god.
South: *Blue sky*
      Netherland of day-god.
East: *Life-blood*
      Scarlet essence.
West: *Women dead of childbirth*
      following in wake of sun, Quetzalcoatl
    Link to world of dead,
      white bone dust.

Moctezuma I followed Itzcóatl's reign and between 1440 and 1468 was responsible for the transformation of Tenochtitlán from the thatched-roof village stage into a structural metropolitan entity. He imported from the southern town of Chalco artisans who used tezontle, a blood-colored stone, and lime-plastered adobe to build the solid foundations and permanent buildings. Moctezuma I also solved the problem of seasonal floods from the slightly higher elevation of Lake Texcoco. Under the direction and advice of his ally, King Netzahualcoyotl of Texcoco, Moctezuma had a ten-mile dike constructed of rubble masonry and stone, dividing the lake in two: the smaller half to the west, surrounding Tenochtitlán, was named Lake of Mexico; the eastern, larger half, retained the name of Lake Texcoco. The previously brackish waters of the Lake of Mexico were replenished by fresh water from the lakes of the south through the narrows of Culhuacán and Mexicaltzingo. In this manner, the basin of saline water was transformed, in the words of Francisco de Garay, into a

TEMPLE PRECINCT, TENOCHTITLÁN.

"fishpond and a home for all sorts of aquatic fowl. Chinampas covered its surface, separated by limpid spaces which were furrowed by swift canoes and all the suburbs of this enchanting capital became flowery orchards."

The city was celebrated for its flowers — dahlias, marigolds and poinsettias, but did not concern itself with the growing of foodstuffs, relying instead on flotillas of pirogues which brought vegetables and maize across the lake from the mainland farming villages.

The four causeways converging into the sacred temple precinct were the arteries leading into the religious heart of the city, the temple precinct which was the nucleus of Tenochtitlán. This huge quadrangular area, 1500 feet on a side, ten times larger than St. Mark's Square in Venice, was completely surrounded by a canal. Enframing the square was a parapet of stone, carved into interlocking serpent motifs (coatepantli), one of the many design features carried over from the Toltecs. Within the enclosure were over seventy structures, all oriented on an east-west axis and all serving a religious function. There were gladiatorial arenas, pools for bathing ceremonies, religious schools (calmecac), sacrificial altars and temples (teocallis), stone ballcourts (tlachtli) where basketball-like games were played, and innumerable pieces of sculpture. The temple of Quetzalcoatl, one of the few circular structures, rose from the center of the square. Twin temples, one dedicated to Tláloc, benign god of rain, the other to Huitzilopochtli, belligerent god of war, crowned the focal point of the temple precinct, the monumental Great Pyramid.

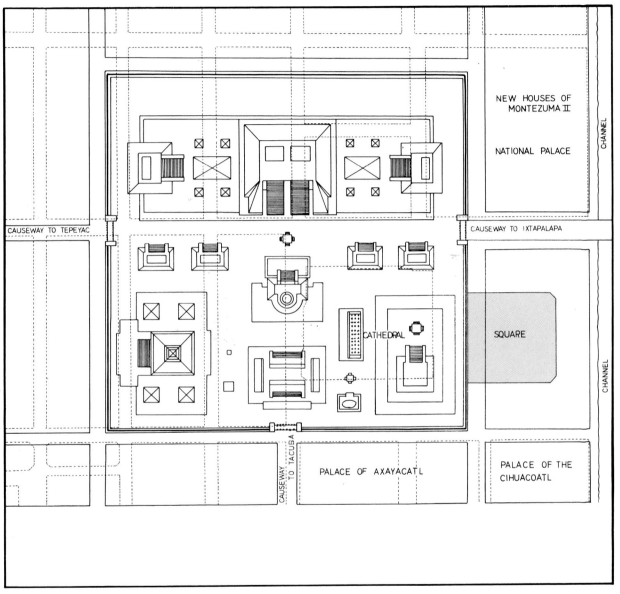

NEW HOUSES OF
MONTEZUMA II

NATIONAL PALACE

CHANNEL

CAUSEWAY TO TEPEYAC

CAUSEWAY TO IXTAPALAPA

CHANNEL

CATHEDRAL

SQUARE

CAUSEWAY TO TACUBA

PALACE OF AXAYACATL

PALACE OF THE
CIHUACOATL

TEMPLE PRECINCT OF TENOCHTITLÁN.

Before its annihilation by the Spaniards, this site was the political and religious nucleus of the Aztec capital. In the plan, present-day structures are superimposed over the original temple precinct. The square in front of the cathedral, although one of the largest in the world, is dwarfed by comparison to the pre-Hispanic layout. Although the national palace covers Moctezuma's houses, the metropolitan cathedral has replaced the temples, and concrete and automobiles have supplanted canals and canoes, the basic function of of the two sites remains the same.

Gran Teocalli
    crucible of our faith
Fulcrum
    bearing the weight of our devotion
to Tláloc and Huitzilopochtli.
The gods
    matrix and vortex of our civilization
preside over everything.
Every thought and act
    from birth to death
a sacred mandate.
Our lives are dedicated to honor and sustain them
    nourish them and give them life
with human blood.
Quetzalcoatl
    life-giver
His blood soaking the bones of the dead
    giving life to a new mankind.
Huitzilopochtli
    sun-warrior
Covering the earth with his heat and light
    dying at dusk, exhausted.
Blood spilling on the altar stone
    revitalizing him for tomorrow's dawn.

Huitzilopochtli
    voracious warrior
heart-hunger quenched by obsidian blade
plunged into up-bowed breast,
    quivering with glory-fear.
                Huitzilopochtli
who led us to this place so long ago.

HUITZILOPOCHTLI.
Codex Borbónicus, adapted from Miguel Covarrubias' painting.

32

The massive, inclined planes of the Great Pyramid contained steps which led to the top, upon which the sacrificial ceremonies took place. Doubtless the monumental size and dynamic configuration of the Great Pyramid created a certain psychological impact conducive to the devastating rituals that took place upon it.

The astonishing fact is that at the time of the Spanish Conquest the Aztecs had not yet reached their cultural apogee, having had only two hundred years of evolution; yet they created Tonochtitlán, with its lavish gardens and temples aided by neither wheel nor beast of burden. It is curious to note that the wheel in hoop form was used in children's toys and in the ceremonial ball games; however, the Aztecs had not yet conceived of its utilitarian potential when the Spaniards arrived.

The sumptuousness of the Aztec capital — its magnificent buildings, broad causeways and slender willow trees reflected on the surrounding water — completely fascinated the Spanish conquerors when they arrived in 1519. After devoting months to a seemingly endless struggle against hostile natives and sweltering jungles, climbing into ever-higher altitudes with no clear idea what would confront them at the summit, the Spaniards were totally unprepared for the visual shock of Tenochtitlán's lofty grandeur.

Cortés's reaction upon his entry into the city was one of frank astonishment. In a letter to his sovereign, the Emperor Charles V, he described Tenochtitlán: "The greatness and the strange and marvelous things of this great city . . . will cause so much wonder, that they will hardly be believed, because even we, who see them with our own eyes, are unable to comprehend them." Bernal Díaz del Castillo was equally impressed and wrote in his memoirs: "We were amazed and said that it was like the enchantments they tell of in the legend of Amadis, on account of the great towers and temples and buildings rising from the water, and all built of masonry. And some of our soldiers even asked whether the things that we saw were not a dream."

Fascination and awe notwithstanding, human frailty and greed prevailed. The regal splendor of Tenochtitlán was doomed. The end came in August, 1521, when after seventy-five days of siege, the Aztecs succumbed to the Spaniards on the broad expanse of Tlatelolco. The invulnerability of Tenochtitlán's watery citadel was finally breached. The Aztec and his monumental capital were destroyed.

The total destruction of Tenochtitlán was, according to Spengler, "the only instance of the violent death of a civilization. This culture did not degenerate step by step, it was not inhibited or disturbed, but crushed in its prime, wiped out like a sunflower decapitated by a passerby with one blow of his stick."

TLÁLOC.
Codex Magliabecchiano, adapted from Miguel Covarrubias' painting.

That night,
        melancholic, devastating night
of horror
        pain
                anguish
                        fire
Gods
        tumbling into space
                our space
Gods
        with their divinity
                broken.
Canals of blood-froth
        lifeless testament of conquest.

Rivulets of blood soaking the tezontle
        venous rock on which our culture rests.

And then the dawn
        dismal dawn of death stench.

Hushed
        our
                dead
                        Tenochtitlán

Dawn
        pale sun illuminates the pallor
                of defeat
and death
        of greatness
                triumph
                        glory.
The gods
        they answer not
except Tláloc
        sending rain
                muted tears
Silence
        echoing the void,
                nothingness.

35

PLAZAS

The Architecture of the Colonial era does not coincide with that which preceded it in pre-Cortesian times. Nevertheless, it mysteriously conserves a strength of space which makes the dimensions of plazas and patios totally different from those built by the Spaniards from whom its form is copied.

—José Villagrán García
Professor and Director
National School of Architecture

MONTE ALBÁN, OAXACA.
Without question, this became one of the world's most remarkable examples of land use. Its site selection and distribution of structures made it Mexico's counterpart of England's Stonehenge and the Acropolis of Greece. The scope and proportion of this pre-Hispanic plaza heralded the direction which the Colonial plazas were to follow.

Photograph by Armando Salas Portugal

As long as towns have existed, man has alloted within them pockets of open space to meet, trade, and communicate with his fellowman. Since their inception, these areas, in Mexico or elsewhere — call them town square, piazza or plaza — have functioned basically in the bringing together of human beings.

In the state of Oaxaca, dating from A.D. 300, stands the extraordinary plaza of Monte Albán. Perched on the pinnacle of a mountain whose peak had been leveled to accommodate its grand dimensions, the plaza of Monte Albán measures 1200 by 600 feet. At the time of its completion it was totally surrounded by structures which faced the square. The totality of this enclosure heightened the sense of communal interaction, a quality which above all others is requisite for the success of a plaza.

One thousand years later the Aztecs produced Tenochtitlán and with it, the Plaza of Tlatelolco, the social and commercial center of the city which drew people, their artifacts, and their produce from all corners of the Empire.

TLATELOLCO. *Courtesy I.N.A.H.*

When the Spaniards first entered Tenochtitlán, Bernal Díaz, fascinated by the spectacle of Tlatelolco wrote:

> ...we were astonished at the number of people and the quantity of merchandise that it contained, and at the good order and control that was maintained, for we had never seen such a thing before. Before reaching the great temple there is a great enclosure of courts... with two walls of masonry surrounding it, and the court itself all paved with very smooth great white flagstones. And where there were not these stones, it was cemented and burnished and all very clean, so that one could not find any dust or a straw in the whole place. ...Some of the soldiers among us who had been in many parts of the world, in Constantinople, and all over Italy, and in Rome, said that so large a marketplace and so well regulated and arranged, they had never beheld before.

After the fall of Tenochtitlán, the Conquerors set about the business of transforming the pagan capital into a proper Christian habitat. To achieve this, Cortés first ordered the methodical destruction of all buildings and temples of Tenochtitlán, obliterating the tangible greatness of the conquered Aztecs. As the city was rebuilt, great blocks of tezontle were torn out of the temples and transformed into new buildings; crushed idols were used to fortify their foundations. Alonso García Bravo, one of Cortés's soldiers described as being a "good geometer," was selected to redesign the city. García Bravo retained the basically cruciform plan of Tenochtitlán, broadening the causeways but maintaining their direction. A cross was drawn on Huitzilopochtli's temple, marking the site for the proposed cathedral of Mexico City. The vast expanse of paving directly in front of the cathedral site was designated for the main square of Mexico City—the Plaza Mayor.

In spite of the brutal transformation of Mexico-Tenochtitlán, the city retained much of the brilliance and color characteristic of Moctezuma's reign. Flowering trees, tabebuia, poincianna, and frangipani were still mirrored in the waterways; gardens continued to flourish, and the stone-rubbed stucco of the houses still shone in the sunlight. Although the Spaniards had begun to drain many of its canals, replacing them with solid streets, Mexico City was called "Great Venice," being larger than its European counterpart. Potable water continued to be channeled in from Chapultepec, producing aqueducts and public fountains which became impressive focal points throughout the city.

Homes and gardens of Spanish design began to emerge, built more from memory than from precise plans and drawings, hence a landscape character evolved with definite European overtones, but one which remained only generically European. The distinctive topographical and climatic conditions, exotic plants, and the personal quality of indigenous labor prevented Mexico City from becoming a replica of Castile.

As new settlements were established throughout the country, King Philip II set forth a series of ordinances specifically citing the manner and direction which the new town was to take. In 1573, he issued a mandate outlining the design and specifications for the plazas or town squares of New Spain as quoted in Stanislawski's *Early Spanish Town Planning in the New World*.

> *. . . The four corners of the plaza face to the four principal winds, because in this way the streets leaving the plaza are not exposed to the principal winds, which would be of great inconvenience.*
> *The plaza should be a rectangle, prolonged so that the length is at least half again as long as the width, because this form is best for celebrations*

La Fuente del Salto del Agua.
Lithograph from *Mexico y Sus Alrededores*, 1856.

Lithograph from *México y Sus Alrededores* 1856.

La Fuente de la Tlaxpana.

with horses, and for any others that are to take place.

The size of the plaza should be proportionate to the populations, taking into consideration that in Indian towns, since they are new and intended to increase, the plaza should be designed with such increase in mind. It should not be less than two hundred feet in width and three hundred feet in length, nor greater than eight hundred feet in length and five hundred and thirty-two in width; a good proportion is the intermediate size of six hundred feet in length and four hundred in width.

All around the plaza and the four principal streets that start from it there should be colonnades because of the great convenience that they offer to the merchants who gather here; the eight streets that leave from the four corners of the plaza are not to have colonnades that would block their juncture with the plaza.

Thus, while Mexican plazas derived from European concepts, their design and size, were decidedly different from their Mediterranean counterparts.

With few exceptions—Bruges and Ypres in Northern Europe, the setting of the cathedral in Sienna, or the Piazza de San Marcos in Venice—European squares were relatively small and irregular in shape, the outcome of centuries of constricted space and accidental design. Plazas of New Spain however were conceived and built with unlimited availability of space, unhampered by pre-existing streets and buildings. The result was a spacious, uncluttered area, geometrically laid out and true to the theoretical ideals of Leone Battista Alberti, the great urbanist of the Renaissance.

Virtually every town and village in New Spain followed the same general pattern. The nucleus of the community was the plaza fronted by the church and flanked on the other three sides by municipal and commercial establishments. In the oldest part of Mexico City, churches mushroomed so profusely that each neighborhood had its plaza, no further than 500 yards from its neighbor.

The plazas were usually paved with cobblestone or stone blocks, surrounded on three sides by arcaded sidewalks (portales) appended to the front of surrounding buildings. The portales protected both merchants and pedestrians from sun and rain; the plaza itself, however, lacked shelter of any kind. This problem was solved in the nineteenth century by the civic-minded Emperor Maximilian of Hapsburg, who introduced the idea of planting trees and flowers throughout the plazas. This innovation was enthusiastically accepted and soon most of the plazas throughout Mexico abounded with greenery. Later in the nineteenth century, bandstands or kiosks were added, as were cast iron or tiled benches and fountains, converting the austere expanses of pavement into parklike areas of green. The introduction of planting in the plazas is the prime legacy left by Maximilian, second only to the elegant layout of the Paseo de la Reforma, the most beautiful, tree-lined boulevard in Mexico City.

Inevitably the technical innovations of the twentieth century made the plaza nearly obsolete. This was especially evident in Mexico City where movie theatres and sports arenas became the popular attraction centers; supermarkets and department stores supplanted most of the open-air markets under the plaza's portales; the combustion engine shortened the distances within the ever-growing city. The plaza was no longer the socioeconomic hub of the community; the neatly trimmed trees and flowers suffered from lack of maintenance, tiles broke and fell from benches, not to be replaced; the fountains were empty and neglected. The irony of this deterioration lies in the fact that the tension and anxiety accompanying the fast pace of the contemporary Mexican Capital cry out for the serenity of the plaza's green open spaces.

In 1967 public conern for the plaza's state of deterioration prompted a series of conferences on the restoration of historically significant sites of this nature.

These discussions resulted in a citywide movement to replant, repave, and refurbish the city's historical plazas. Church facades, fountains, and monuments were repaired and restored with a conscious effort to maintain their original character and design.

Two noteworthy examples are within the central business district of Mexico City. The Plaza de la Santa Veracruz, across from de Alameda Park on

PLAZA DE LA SANTA VERACRUZ, MÉXICO, D. F.

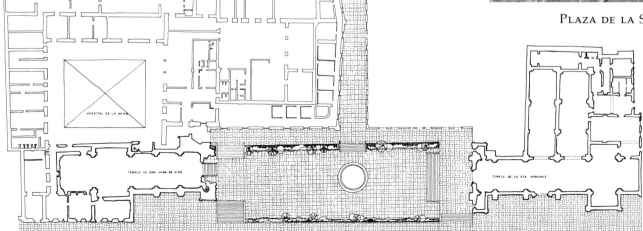

Courtesy Artes de México

43

Hidalgo Street, traces its beginnings to the sixteenth century, with the establishment of the church of Santa Veracruz—third oldest parish of Mexico-Tenochtitlán. The site in front of the church was used originally as a cemetary for indigents, and not until later as a plaza in the traditional sense.

In the seventeenth century, layout of the plaza was completed with the construction of the church-hospital complex of San Juan de Dios on the west end of the plaza. Thus the plaza, nestled between its two churches is uniquely sheltered and intimate.

Because of the marshy subsoil of this particular area, the buildings began to sink. Throughout the years clumsy attempts were made to bolster the foundations, altering their original proportions. Crude coats of plaster and paint were added intermittently, rudely obliterating the fine detailing of both churches.

In 1967 the present restoration was begun. The exteriors of both churches were restored in their entirety. Crumbling stone and stucco were replaced, layers of plaster removed to expose the original stonework of the church of Santa Veracruz and the whimsical mudéjar patterns of molded plaster of the facade of San Juan de Dios.

Since the original grade of the churches had sunk more than six feet, the plaza was lowered to reveal the original proportions of the buildings. The result was fortunate in that the sound of traffic on Hidalgo Street above is now muffled, the cacophony and bustle of the city subdued. The plaza was newly paved, cast iron benches and railings added, planting introduced and lighting installed. The surrounding buildings repainted in neutral hues and utility cables buried.

The plaza of San Fernando is equally significant and rich in history. The church was established in the seventeenth century by Franciscan missionaries. Like the Plaza de la Santa Veracruz, San Fernando's plaza was also used as a cemetary until 1836 when this use was outlawed by the Municipal Council. The brothers moved the cemetary to the side of the church where subsequently it became the Panteón of Famous Men, its most illustrious occupant being Benito Juárez.

Urban sprawl crept insidiously around the original plaza of San Fernando. The plaza ultimately was destroyed, giving way to a street which sliced through its original block of open space. The neighborhood

PLAZA DE SAN FERNANDO, MÉXICO, D. F.

fell into disrepair and decay. Until 1967 the district was dying—a victim of senseless urban rot.

Since then the offensive street has been removed, the plaza redesigned and the neighborhood restored to life.

A central avenue of paving bordered by jets of water frames the front of the church. Small squares of paving jut into planting beds, giving them the feeling of enclosure and privacy. Flowers abound around the fountains, the plaza is full of pigeons, children, and flower vendors. The plaza, and the neighborhood which surrounds it, are alive again.

The importance of the restoration movement was expressed in a speech by the mayor of Mexico City, Alfonso Corona del Rosal:

We are confronted with new problems and must find an answer to the new demands which the growth of the modern city imposes on us. . . . However, in addition to these demands is another, no less important: that of preserving the living symbols of our history, our struggle and the hopes of our ancestors; symbols whose value cannot be expressed in monetary terms.

PLAZA DE LA CONSTITUCIÓN, MÉXICO, D. F.
Popularly called the Zócalo, the main plaza of Mexico City has undergone several transformations since its occupancy by Aztec priests. It has been used variously as a tree-lined promenade for the fashionable, as parade ground for the patriotic, as battleground for revolutionaries, and until the 1970s, a terrifying arena for pedestrians. Traffic then was re-routed and the Zócalo became once again a place for people, a fresh-air terminal for the "Metro" or subway which passes underneath.

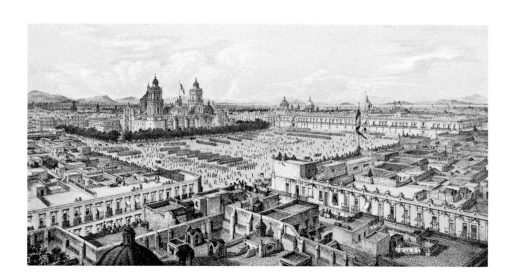

QUERÉTARO, QUERÉTARO.
An ornate kiosk, focal point of most plazas, dominates the center of this one. On weekends and holidays the plaza pulsates with life. Around the kiosk, townspeople promenade and dance to the oomphas and clarions of its musicians.

GUANAJUATO, GUANAJUATO.
Diminutive in size and irregular in shape, the plaza departs from traditional dimensions and configuration. The mountainous topography of Guanajuato dictated this break from the norm, a delightful indulgence to the characteristics of the land. One of several plazas which abound throughout the city, it compensates in charm and intimacy for what it lacks in size and regularity.

TAXCO, GUERRERO.
The plaza serves as foreground
for the baroque splendor of the
church of Santa Prisca, revealing
its sumptuous architecture and
reinforcing its importance to a
people in whose lives religion
occupies a major role. This is
the ultimate function of the
plaza—the bringing together
of architecture and humanity.

Photograph by Armando Salas Portugal

TOLUCA, MEXICO.
A plaza in the purest sense, according to the specifications set forth by Philip II, it is surrounded by civic and commercial buildings, complete with arcaded *portales*. The great fountain dominates the square, its water introducing the only natural element.

XOCHITLÁN, PUEBLA.
Nor need the plaza be grandiose and imposing. Tiny Xochitlán, tucked in the mountains of Puebla, embraces its placita. This miniscule and understated gem, overlooking the village from the top of a hill, reflects the peace, humility, and simple life of its inhabitants.

Photograph by Armando Salas Portugal

ALAMOS, SONORA.
Archetypal people-places of Mexican towns, plazas emerge throughout the entire country. Alamos was one of the northernmost outposts of Colonial Spain; because of its isolation, the twentieth century has bypassed it, leaving its Colonial essence undisturbed.

Photograph by Armando Salas Portugal

GUADALAJARA, JALISCO.
Instead of facing one great
plaza, the Cathedral of Guadalajara is flanked on its sides by
four plazas, each articulating a
different image. An eighteenth-
century bandstand with cary-
atids used as supports is the
focal point of one; on another,
fountains resound with cascades of water.

Photograph by Armando Salas Portugal

52

The Cathedral, one of the most imposing structures of the city, can be appreciated particularly for the outdoor space which surrounds it. The plazas are essential for the exposure of its beauty.

Photograph by Armando Salas Portugal

53

PARKS

Nature is the basis,
but man is the goal.

— George Santayana

Lithograph from *México y Sus Alrededores* 1856.

CHAPULTEPEC PARK.

ALTHOUGH CONCEIVED AND CREATED BY MAN, the urban environment is an unnatural entity. Because of this, the moment arrives in the life of every man in which he yearns to retreat, to come in contact with something other than that which is man-made. In the serenity of the forested park, the surrounding greenery brings relief from a mechanized world. This relief—as essential to the life of the city as is commerce and industry—would, in its absence, result in a sterile conglomerate of steel, concrete, asphalt—and desolate humanity.

These apertures of nature are the city's defense against the encroachment of land development and traffic. Here the city does not intrude, but is held at bay by a natural barrier of trees. Nor is it solely the sentinel of greenery which holds "progress" in abeyance. It is that frequently forgotten yearning in all mankind to reach back and identify with nature.

Once established, a park attains a rather special aura, a personal identity with those who have walked its paths, smelled its fragrances, listened to its sounds. Perhaps no other recreational body crosses as many social, economical, and age barriers. A park evokes as many responses as the myriad of people who enjoy it. Whatever its attraction— intimate bower of lovers, playground of children,

dog-run of apartment dweller, meeting place of octogenarian—the ultimate bond is a momentary respite from urban pressures—noise, smog, anxiety. It is that last stronghold, the link with nature. To deny a city its parks is to deny it life, render it sterile.

In this sense, Mexico's urban scene is very much alive, with green open spaces abounding throughout the cities. The Mexican's innate love of plants, a tradition which has been manifested for countless generations, is evident in the quality and treatment of Mexican parks.

The most notable and historically significant park is Mexico City's Chapultepec, the oldest park in America. One of the most beautiful parks in the world, Chapultepec is Mexico's answer to London's Hyde Park and Paris' Bois de Boulogne. The tremendous ahuehuete trees which shade the park so regally date from the middle of the fifteenth century, their planting having been attributed to King Netzahualcoyotl, the poet-ruler of Texcoco. Before the Conquest, Chapultepec "Grasshopper Hill" was the summer haven for Aztec sovereigns, its menagerie of beasts protected by Imperial decree and its pools and terraces carefully designed to take advantage of the panorama of Tenochtitlán.

In 1530, King Philip II of Spain decreed that

Chapultepec was to be dedicated to the City of Mexico for the enjoyment of her people in perpetuity. In 1554 the second Spanish viceroy, Don Luis de Velasco, dedicated the top of the hill to the Christian hermitage of Saint Xavier. The surrounding forest was dedicated to the Emperor, Charles V, and was used as a hunting and recreational site for the viceregal courts during the sixteenth and seventeenth centuries.

In 1785, on the site of the old hermitage, Viceroy Don Bernardo de Galvez constructed a fort which in 1841 was turned into a military academy. The young cadets were immortalized as national heroes in 1847 when they gave their lives defending the fort against the invading American Army during the Mexican War.

During the French Intervention in 1864, the fort was transformed into the imperial residence of Maximilian. Buildings and gardens were reconstructed to suit the Emperor's European taste. The surrounding gardens of the castle emerged as an exercise in seventeenth century landscape architecture, with characteristic marble loggias and balustrades, formal parterres and fountained nymphs.

Beyond the castle the design of Chapultepec might be described as "rambling Mexicanesque."

Its footpaths and equestrian trails meander throughout the area, converging at unexpected intervals, diverging once more in different directions. Its informal design enhances the natural beauty of the gigantic trees. One feels that man's presence is purely accidental.

One is never out of sight or sound of water. The aquatic displays of Chapultepec are as characteristic of the park as its ahuehuete trees. Waterworks range from torrential displays of hydraulic expertise, such as Netzahualcoyotl's fountain, to subtle, understated filaments of water such as emerge from Don Quixote's fountain at the end of the Path of the Poets.

Within the confines of Chapultepec are a remarkable zoological display, an amusement park boasting the world's largest roller coaster, several theaters, the municipal auditorium and the city's finest museums, notably the Museum of History, the Museum of Fine Arts, and the spectacular Museum of Anthropology.

The vastness of the park is such that the presence of these structures is unobtrusive. If one chooses, he is alone with nature, oblivious to the recreational and cultural activity which is taking place beyond.

The Alameda Central in the heart of Mexico City is an excellent example of a midtown park or public promenade. Its forty acres are as compact and formal as Chapultepec is huge and rambling. In 1592, under Viceroy Luis de Velasco, the city council ordered allocation of an outdoor site for recreational use. The old Indian market, the Tianguiz de San Hipólito in the center of the city, was chosen as a suitable spot. The small park was planted with poplars and named Alameda—*alamo* being the Spanish word for these trees. The park was dedicated to the public in 1618. In 1775 it was expanded to twice its original size under orders from Viceroy Marquis de Croix. This act created quite a controversy since extension of the Alameda would occupy the site of the Quemadero, a stone platform upon which public executions were carried out during the Inquisition. The substitution of a public promenade for the Quemadero incurred such ire on the part of the Holy Office that the audacious Marquis nearly met his own fiery doom on the same disputed site. The Marquis overrode the wrath of the Inquisitors, however, and the Alameda Central was redesigned and completed.

Mexico has continued to add open recreational spaces for the enrichment and health of her cities. By the 1970s, in the Federal District alone there were 288 parks and public gardens—a total of more than 12 million square miles of green areas whose shrubs and trees give shade and oxygen, mitigating the harshness, noise, and pollution of the surrounding city.

With little exception the nations's parks are basically patterned after Chapultepec and the Alameda. Large municipal parks echo Chapultepec's informal forest and meandering paths. Small mid-town parks throughout the country not only retain the symmetric design of Mexico City's Alameda but often bear the same name, whether they are shaded by poplars or not.

The most notable aspect of Mexico's parks, however, lies not so much in their beauty or originality of design, but in the manner in which they are utilized. It is the people which make them extraordinary.

From early morning until late evening, the parks are never empty—but alive with lovers, children, sidewalk philosophers, and balloon men resplendent with their kaleidoscopic masses of color.

The lively presence of people not only complements the natural beauty of parks but it is their raison d'être. Not here the pathetic vandal-plagued parks of other places, but parks enjoyed, used, and appreciated to the fullest.

Chapultepec Park, Mexico, D. F.
Footpaths such as the aptly named "Path of the Poets" and "Path of the Philosophers" meander through the forest. The ahuehuetes have endured the passage of time in spite of the increasing scarcity of ground water due to the continued drainage of the subsoil. Branches no longer droop with moss but continue to offer a natural canopy for man.

DON QUIXOTE FOUNTAIN, CHAPULTEPEC PARK, MÉXICO, D. F.
One of the most intimate and delightful spots of Mexico City is this secluded fountain at the end of the "Path of the Poets." A single jet sends a slender thread of water to the miniature pool below. Facing the fountain are four curved benches, their surface covered with tile, each one depicting a different scene from Cervantes' "Don Quixote." Across from each other are statuettes, one of Don Quixote, the other of Sancho Panza. The colossal girth of the ahuehuete trunks emphasizes the subtlety and delicacy of this understated gem.

Perched atop a hill overlooking the park, the Castle has witnessed the history and transfiguration of the city. Converted for use as a museum, it has in the past housed the former rulers of Mexico. The garden and intricate gate of cast iron lace are Europe transformed.

CHAPULTEPEC CASTLE, MÉXICO, D. F.

A seemingly interminable allée of water gushes and spills in a Mexican variation on Italy's Villa d'Este. The long sweep of the fountain compels the eye to follow its course towards the monument to King Netzahualcoyotl at the opposite end of the mall.

NETZAHUALCOYOTL'S FOUNTAIN, CHAPULTEPEC PARK, MÉXICO, D. F.

Photograph by Armando Salas Portugal

Complementing the centuries-old ahuehuetes in the park's interior, a phalanx
of ash trees provides a buffer between
park and thoroughfare. Smooth paths of
compacted earth and sand lead into
Chapultepec's interior, leaving traffic
and city momentarily forgotten.

CHAPULTEPEC PARK, MÉXICO, D. F.

Components of quasi-infinite stone, water and trees make up the spacious pedestrian mall on the western half of the park. The presence of water which pervades the park never allows one to be out of its visual or audible reach.

MALL FOUNTAIN,
CHAPULTEPEC PARK,
MÉXICO, D. F.

From *México y Sus Alrededores*, 1856.

ALAMEDA PARK AS SEEN FROM A BALLOON IN 1856.

With the western addition of the Quemadero, the Alameda had nearly reached its final dimensions. Its design is pure European baroque with diagonal paths slicing symmetrically through the park, interrupted at regular intervals by circular glorietas punctuated by fountains. Sometime later the symmetry of the park was knocked askew when the western half was broadened to run parallel to Hidalgo Street on the north.

ALAMEDA PARK, MÉXICO, D. F.
Taken from García Conde's plan, 1792.

From *México y Sus Alrededores*, 1856.   ALAMEDA PARK.

The popular appeal of the gardens and fountains of the Alameda is universal. Since 1618, rich and poor, old and young have sought respite from the commotion of the surrounding city. The suspended tranquility of mythological muses and nymphs enclosed in sheets of water creates a nonaggressive dichotomy with the surrounding rush of Mexico City traffic. Time stands still in the Alameda.

Photograph by Armando Salas Portugal

A bronze Venus from another era transports the Alameda back in time. One is ever-conscious but never disturbed by the contrast between past epochs and the present. For almost four centuries the park has offered a natural haven for its people — Emperor and commoner alike. Its original bower of trees has died and been replaced, nymph-topped fountains have been added, deleted and modified, according to the tastes of time. Yet, its denizens remain the same — those in search of momentary respite from the artifacts of civilization. The twentieth century envelops this natural bastion of nostalgia; yet its charm transcends any vestige of anachronism.

ALAMEDA PARK, MEXICO, D. F.

Alameda Park, México, D. F.

SAN LUIS, POTOSÍ.

As basic an element as trees and shrubbery, water is an ever-present component in Mexican parks, its ubiquitous sound and motion appearing in fountains, pools, and lakes. Here the circular system of jets surrounds the central kiosk which is connected to the mainland by a bridge.

PARQUE ALCALDE, GUADALAJARA, JALISCO.

Notable among Mexican hydraulic displays is the array of fountains in Guadalajara's Parque Alcalde. Providing a spectacular backdrop for the lake and park below, water leaps in rhythmical progression from the fountain's summit, ultimately crashing into the lake in torrential cascades.

These gardens were originally laid out by José de la Borda, a self-made millionaire whose enterprises in silver mining during the eighteenth century extended to the northern state of Sonora. The grounds of his estate were re-established by Maximilian in the nineteenth century and transformed into an inland Miramar. Here was escape from Mexico City and the dreary business of politics and intrigue. The arcaded pavilion, encircled on the plan, overlooks a small lake in which the Empress and her entourage rowed to the landing on the lake's opposite extreme. Mango and papaya trees abound but according to legend no birds sing — a token to the memory of this tragic couple. A pastoral and evocative quality infuses the gardens. Pools and flower beds have not been kept up and have fallen into decay — an aura of melancholy pervades.

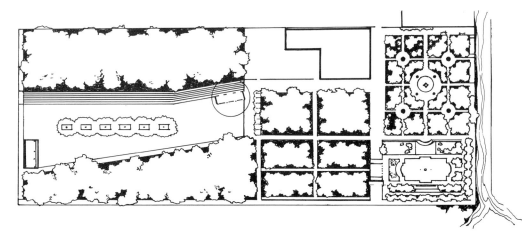

BORDA GARDENS, CUERNAVACA, MORELOS.

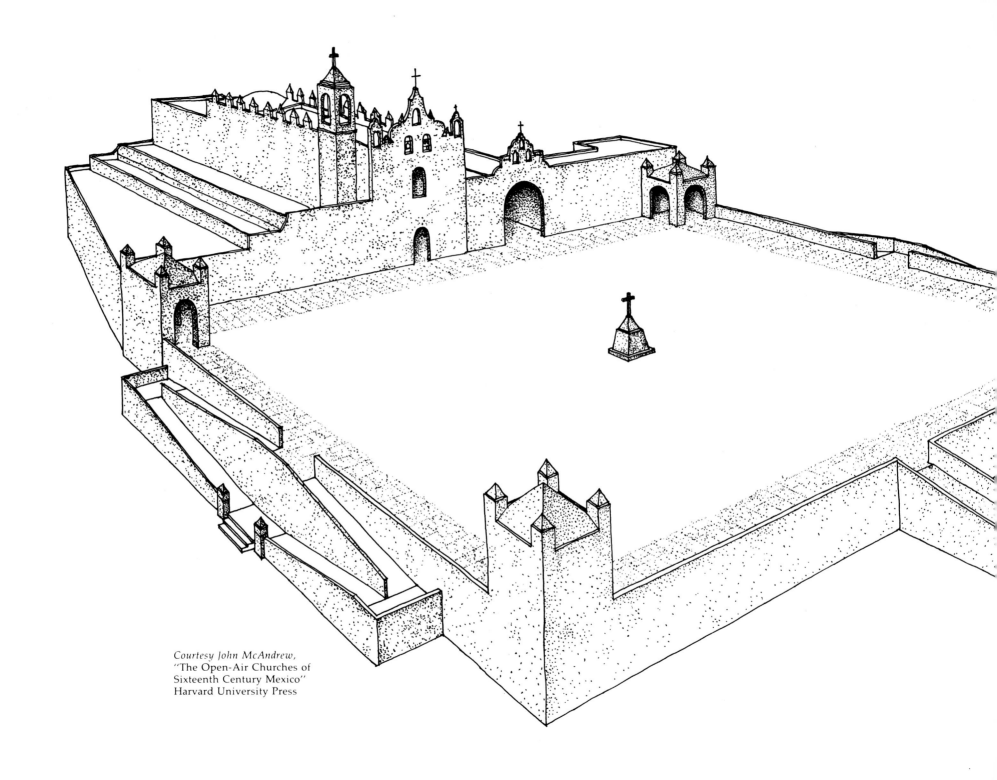

Courtesy John McAndrew,
"The Open-Air Churches of
Sixteenth Century Mexico"
Harvard University Press

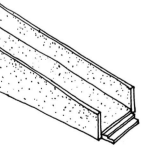

TWO

THE VIEW FROM WITHIN

Bosque del Contador.
Courtesy National Geographic Society:
Photograph by Justin Locke

THE ROOTS OF ANAHUAC

Will I leave only this—
Like the flowers that wither?
Will nothing last in my name—
Nothing of my fame here on earth?
At least flowers!
At least songs!

—Canciones de Huejotzingo

It is disconcerting that the Aztecs, with their inordinate blood thirst and brutality, displayed such keen affinity and sensitivity for gardens and plants. This was remarkably evident throughout Tenochtitlán —in the cypress-crowned chinampas, in the homes of its inhabitants and in the palaces of its rulers. Reverence for green, growing things extended even into their religion, represented in the personage of the deity, Xochipilli, "Prince of Flowers," symbolized by a figure decorated with butterflies and flowers, carrying a staff impaled with a human heart. Flower mania extended even to the battlefield, in the so-called "flower wars," whose sole purpose was the capturing of prisoners, referred to as "flowers," and later sacrificed to the gods.

Gardens and plants played such an important part in Aztec life that in the vocabulary there was a definite catalogue of garden types, Xochitla, "flower place," was the basic name for garden; xochitepanyo was a walled garden; the pleasure garden for the ruling class was xochitecpancalli, "flower palace," and humble Indian garden was xochichinancalli, "flower-place enclosed by cane fence." This affinity with plants was carried over into the very existence of the city which relied on plant roots for the stability of its island foundations.

Aztec garden design reached its climax in the mid-fifteenth century, coinciding with the similarly designed Renaissance gardens across the Atlantic. Although an ocean separated these gardens and no

XOCHIPILLI.
Codex Magliabecchiano, adapted from Miguel Covarrubias' painting.

76

human contact had been established between the continents, the approach to landscape design was singularly alike—dramatic usage of water, monumental outdoor sculpture and a constant adherence to symmetry.

By this time the struggle for dominance was over and the empire flourished. The palace gardens of King Netzahualcoyotl on the northeast extreme of Lake Texcoco were outstanding, reflecting the astute engineering and artistic brilliance of their owner and designer.

Netzahualcoyotl's interest in botany was extensive and resulted in his having highly detailed drawings of plant specimens painted on the walls of his palace. These drawings were extremely accurate and later of great scientific value for the sixteenth-century Spanish botanist, Dr. Francisco Hernández, sent to Mexico by Philip II in 1570 to explore the flora of New Spain.

Netzahualcoyotl's cypress garden, the Bosque del Contador, reached magnificent proportions. Constructed on a ten-acre site, the garden was enclosed by a double row of over 1,000 ahuehuetes, or bald cypress trees. Lush gardens of flowers and shrubs between paved walkways were contained within the border of the cypress. An avenue of these same gigantic trees led out of the grove to a dike behind which was a deep, oblong pool, bordered by another circular grove of trees. This constant adherence to fomal geometric shapes, found in all Aztec design and carried over into religious symbolism, clearly reflected a proclivity for environmental order and for control.

Netzahualcoyotl's botanical activities culminated in his garden villa of Texcotzinco. On that magnificent site, built on a hill of rose-colored porphyry, overlooking the panorama of Lake Texcoco and Tenochtitlán, dramas were enacted, poetry was read, and philosophy was debated. In the terrace garden, an aqueduct brought water to an eight-foot pool or cistern on the summit of the hill. Stuccoed channels from the pool were distributed throughout the hill, carrying water which cascaded to the rocks and plants below. The terrace, carved out of the living rock on the face of the hill, was enclosed by a low parapet allowing a spectacular view of the lake.

One of the most fascinating among Aztec gardens was that of Moctezuma in Iztapalapa, seven miles to the south of Tenochtitlán on the southern shore of the lake. It was a two-storied structure with pools and terraced gardens on both floors. Cortés described it in a letter to Charles V:

Within the orchard is a great square pool of fresh water, very well constructed with sides of handsome masonry, around which runs a walk of well-laid pavement of tiles, so wide that four persons can walk abreast on it and 400 paces square, making in all 1600 paces. On the other side of this promenade toward the walls of the garden are hedges of lattice work made of cane, behind which are all sorts of plantations of trees and aromatic herbs. The pool contains many fish and different kinds of water fowl.

IZTAPALAPA.
Brian L. Rothman

Writing about the same garden, Bernal Díaz describes it:

...We went to the orchard and garden, which was such a wonderful thing to see and walk in, that I was never tired of looking at the diversity of trees, and noting the scent which each one had, and the paths full of roses and flowers, and the many fruit trees and native roses, and the pond of fresh water. There was another thing to observe, that the great canoes were able to pass into the garden from the lake through an opening that had been made so that there was no need for their occupants to land. And all was cemented and very splendid with many kinds of stone [monuments] with pictures on them, which gave much to think about. Then the birds of many kinds and breeds which came into the pond. I say again that I stood looking at it and thought that never in the world would there be discovered other lands such as these. ...Of all these wonders that I then beheld, today all is overthrown and lost, nothing left standing.

The old soldier was obviously enchanted with the loveliness of Iztapalapa. It should be mentioned, however, that roses were unknown to Mexico at that time. Díaz's "roses" were no doubt native flowers the names of which he did not know.

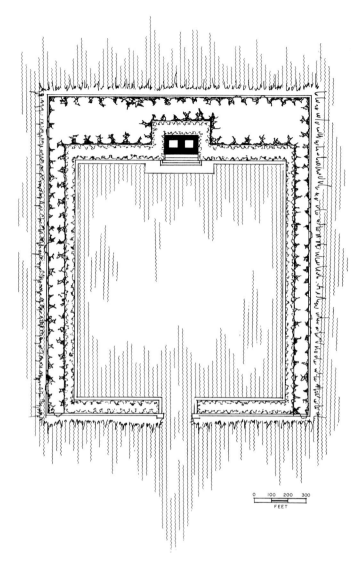

Moctezuma's garden villa incorporated the water of the surrounding lakes into the heart of the garden. Canoes, entering through the gateway, flowed through the beauty of the enclosed lagoon to reach the terraced entrance of the palace.

Moctezuma's palace, in Tenochtitlán, across the canal from the temple precinct, served both a religious and administrative function since he was both ruler and deity. The interiors of the rooms, were starkly elegant, contrasting with the organic lavishness of the gardens. Cortés describes the palace as having

a beautiful terrace-garden with green arbors overhanging it, of which the marbles and tiles were of jasper, beautifully worked. It had ten pools of water, in which were kept all the many and diverse breeds of waterfowl found in these parts; ... for the sea birds too, there were pools of salt water; ... for those of the rivers and lakes, there was fresh water, which for the sake of cleanliness, they renewed at certain times by means of pipes ... Over each pool for these birds, there were beautifully decorated galleries, balconies, and corridors, where Moctezuma came to amuse himself by watching them.

Bernal Díaz also praised it in writing—

We must not forget the gardens of flowers and sweet-scented trees, and the many kinds that there were of them and the arrangement of them and the walks and the ponds and tanks of fresh water where the water entered at one end and flowed out of the other; and the baths which he had there and the variety of small birds that nested in the branches, and the medicinal and useful herbs that were in the gardens. It was a wonder to see, and to take care of it there were many gardeners. Everything was made in masonry and well cemented, baths, and walks and closets and apartments like summerhouses where they danced and sang.

The Aztec emperor had several villas outside the city which, according to the Spanish historians, were even more sumptuous than his city residence. Moctezuma's summer retreat was perched high on Chapultepec hill, on the western shore of Lake Texcoco. The hill was thickly forested with ahuehuetes which sheltered the Emperor's extensive zoological menagerie. A moat surrounded the forest, preventing the animals' escape. Dr. Cervantes de Salazar, in his "Dialogues" written in 1554, writes of terraces cascading greenery throughout the hill. From these terraces Moctezuma was able to enjoy the spectacular panorama of his watery capital with its backdrop of snowcapped volcanoes.

The most significant of all Moctezuma's gardens was Huastepec, the world's first tropical botanic garden, established during the reign of Moctezuma I, between 1440 and 1468. His fascination for plants led Moctezuma I to import the rarest and most exotic tropical plant specimens from the far corners of his empire. He demanded also that native gardeners from each locale accompany the plants and remain in Huastepec to care and tend for them. Cortés described Huastepec in superlatives: "the finest, pleasantest and largest that ever was seen, having a circumference of two leagues . . . it certainly filled one with admiration to see the grandeur and exquisite beauty of this entire orchard." The historian Torquemada supplements these descriptions by writing that not only was the garden full of flowers, groves of trees and pavilions, but that there were "several large rocks on which were bowers and oratories and observatories with the steps leading to them cut in the solid rock." Moctezuma II had continued to care for Huastepec, enlarging the gardens and adding to the collection of plants. Dr. Hernández also visited Huastepec during his botanical expedition and reported to his sovereign about the vast array of unique tropicals.

The hillside and palace gardens of the Aztecs reflect the highly sensuous nature of their owners— in the ubiquitous sight and sound of water, in the perfume of the myriad of herbs and flowers, and in the spectacular panorama of the Valley of Anáhuac below. Small wonder then that the Spaniards, though conquerors, were themselves captivated.

ATRIOS

To walk into these patios is something to make one praise God.
— Father Gerónimo Mendieta

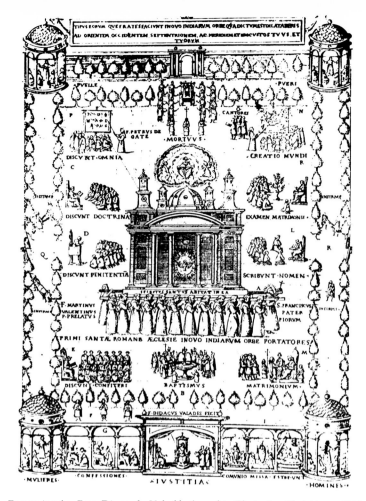

Engraving by Fray Diego de Valadés from his Rhetorica Christiana, 1579.
Courtesy Peabody Museum, Harvard.

THE ARCHETYPAL ATRIO AND ITS ACTIVITIES.

The monks fulfilled a complete range of social and religious services within the perimeter of the atrio. In the corners, the posas serve as religious discussion centers, women on one side, men on the other. Top center shows the atrio gate with a funeral procession taking place in front of it. In the center, monks are in the midst of a procession celebrating the Feast of Pentecost. Surrounding the procession are several instruction classes. The Sacraments of Matrimony, Baptism and Penance are being administered in the bottom vignettes. Within the tree-lined paths, the sick are being brought in for treatment.

PERHAPS THE MOST NOTABLE, certainly the most original innovation in Mexican landscape architecture during the Viceregal Period came through the efforts of the mendicant friars during their missionary crusade of the sixteenth century.

In her will, Queen Isabella had expressed a strong desire that no effort be spared to Christianize New Spain. In accordance with this wish, her successors, Charles V and Philip II made the conversion of Mexico one of their paramount objectives. This task of educating and converting the Indian to Catholicism was delegated to the mendicant orders. The Franciscans, by far the most influential of these groups, were the first to arrive in 1524, followed by the Dominicans in 1526 and the Augustinians in 1533. As the friars arrived they soon spread out to the rural areas of the country establishing almost eighty monasteries by 1550. The magnitude of the conversions must be noted; it was no gradual process but a torrent — an avalanche — of baptisms, numbering in the millions. Fray Juan de Zumárraga, Mexico's first bishop, claimed that by 1531, just ten years after the fall of Tenochtitlán, 1,500,000 Indians had been converted.

Having no professional architects nor accurate plans to rely on, the friars designed and constructed their so-called fortress-monasteries, from memory of European examples, to conform to their immediate and local needs. The term "fortress" is owing in most part to the visual quality of these battlemented and massive structures. The merlons and crenellated parapets which crowned the walls of the monastery complexes were introduced more as a decorative element than as a means of actual defense.

The monasteries of the mendicant friars were not monastic retreats as were those in Europe but were the bases of operation for active missionaries in the field. The monastary establishments consisted of three main parts; the church, the atrio, which was a huge forecourt facing the church, and the monastery building which housed the friars.

Although they never were exact copies or replicas of Spanish architecture, both the monastery and the church were consciously intended to resemble their European counterparts. Conversely, the atrio in front of the church, along with its architectural components, was a totally original feature, having no European antecedents but employed as a solution to the particular spatial needs of the friars and their congregations.

As the number of converts became staggering, it soon became evident that only churches of cathedral-like proportions could accommodate the enormous congregations. The friars were obviously

The site plan of Atlatláuhcan, is as typical as any of the monastery complexes of the sixteenth century. The 370 by 270 foot atrio, except for the omission of the olive trees which continue to shade it, illustrates the standard components — elevated gateway, surrounding wall, corner posas, and open chapel. The site departs from the norm in the exclusion of the familiar atrio cross, and in the addition of a low wall which follows the perimeter of the outer barrier. The small ambulatory wall emphasised the processional route, leading from posa to posa. This not only articulated the circulation path but reinforced the configuration of the atrio's design.

Courtesy John McAndrew, "The Open-Air Churches of Sixteenth Century Mexico", Harvard University Press.

incapable of building such churches. Faced with this spatial dilemma, the friars developed the concept of the atrio, a huge open area capable of containing thousands, even tens of thousands, at one time. Not only was the spatial problem solved but the atrio overcame a psychological block as well. The Indian, accustomed to worshipping outdoors in the tremendous open spaces in front of his teocallis undoubtedly felt cramped and claustrophobic in an enclosed church. The atrio, however, spacious and open to the sky, had a striking similarity to the pre-colonial religious site, and the Indian simply felt at home there. Thus, the transition to Christianity was greatly facilitated by the familiarity of the surroundings. The atrio, usually paved in native tradition of stucco burnished with smooth stones, was punctuated by a rhythmical pattern of trees. Besides providing shade, the avenue of trees indicated the pattern of circulation during services and processions. Neat garden plots were often included, their everblooming flowers noted with pleasure by Father Juan de Torquemada who had never seen such a thing in Spain. Father Gerónimo Mendieta, describing the atrio, wrote:

> All the monasteries in New Spain have a large walled patio in front of the church. . . . The old men keep these patios swept and clean, and usually they are adorned with trees set in orderly rows. In the hot country there are alternate rows of cypress and orange trees, and in the temperate and cold regions there are cypress and pepper trees from Peru which stay green all year. To walk into these patios is something to make one praise God.

Not until the seventeenth century was the term "atrio" coined to distinguish it from the cloistered patio which was totally different in concept and design.

Once the monasteries were established, towns and villages sprang and blossomed around them. The hub of these new communities was the church and with it, its enclosed atrio. Normally a plaza was designed in front of the church and atrio, with one of its peripheral streets separating the two. Thus a great pool of greenery was created in the center of the town, a great green space, serving a twofold purpose for the people which inhabited it—one for religious activity, the other for social and commercial use.

The atrio was the only place in the New World planted with olive trees. These were generally forbidden for fear that their cultivation on a large scale would upset the balance of trade with Spain. Because of this, olive oil never became a staple in Mexican cuisine in spite of the ideal climatic conditions. The ban on olive trees was not enforced in the atrios, however, until the latter part of the sixteenth century. Some of the trees still survive, notably in the atrios of Huexotla, Sta. Cruz Atoyac and Atlatláhuacan, their four hundred years of existence evident in the gnarled and twisted branches which yet sprout with silver-green foliage.

The size of the atrios varied: an approximate average would be about 300 feet, as large as a football field, normally rectangular, but sometimes taking an L shape, with one extremity wrapped around one side of the church.

Since there were never enough friars per flock and these few were allowed to celebrate only one Mass a day, the huge atrio enabled thousands of worshippers to attend each servce. By saying Mass in the open-air atrios, the friars were in effect breaking ecclesiastical canon which emphatically forbade the celebration of Mass anywhere but in a consecrated, enclosed building. The atrios were blessed, but save for the cemetery plot within them, could not actually be consecrated. Some atrios included an open chapel (capilla abierta), an architectural appendage built onto an exterior wall of the church; even these could not be consecrated since they were not an enclosed structure but open to the air on one side, usually supported only by arches. Nevertheless, the friars continued to teach, administer the Sacraments and say Mass, despite

TEPOZTLÁN, MORELOS.
Founded about 1575 by the Dominicans, the monastery of Tepoztlán contains a near proto-type of the atrios of this period. The wide stone steps leading to the atrio recall the stairs leading to the teocallis, evoking a sensation of entering upon sacred grounds. The posa, one of four in the atrio of this Dominican establishment, served as a prayer station during religious processions (posar: to pause). The architectural detailing indicates the rare presence of a profes-sional architect. Francisco Becerra who visited Mexico between 1575 and 1580 may have been the architect, although there is no proof.

Courtesy John McAndrew, "The Open-Air Churches of Sixteenth Century Mexico" Harvard University Press.

the fact that in doing so they risked accusations of unorthodoxy and even heresy from the religious hierarchy in Europe.

A great wall surrounded the monastery complexes, the top of which was usually punctuated by a staccato rhythm of merlons, giving the site its appearance of a battlemented fortress. The atrio was usually on the western side of the church with gardens and orchards on the other three sides. The surrounding wall enclosing the entire monastery area was built on a grand scale; at Xochimilco, for example, the wall reached twelve feet in height and totaled 1500 linear feet. Sometimes an arcaded belfry (espadaña), taller than the wall and pierced with arched openings on which bells could be hung, was incorporated into the wall. The entrance to the atrio consisted of a large arcaded gateway which linked the secular world to the sacred. As a rule, the gateways show no evidence of cuttings in the stone jambs for the attachment of gates or doors, indicating that these remained open to any who wished to enter, further suggesting that the monastery complexes were not designed for defensive purposes.

Single-celled, covered oratories (posas) frequently stood in the corners of the atrio. These structures, ten to twelve feet square, were large enough only for a friar and a covey of altar boys. These were used as prayer stations on special feast days, functioning as chapels as the procession made its way around the atrio. The origin of the posa goes back to pre-Colonial times and the native proclivity toward flowers. Aztec ritual often called for processions with the participants carrying cane reeds and wearing crowns of flowers. After the Conversion, flower-carrying processions persisted, with the natives making flowered canopies and altars to venerate a patron saint.

The stone posas evolved from these flower-altars and became a permanent feature in the atrio. Even today, on special liturgical feast days, posas are lavishly decorated with streamers and carpets of flowers. The design of the posas, however, comes from European antecedents, namely the ciboria, or canopied altar, housing the consecrated Host in European churches. Although the ciboria were found only inside churches and were supported by columns instead of arches, the similarity of purpose and design is striking enough to link the two.

The friars recognized the Indian's inclination to ritual and ceremony, a tendency which surpassed even Catholic proclivity towards pomp and pageantry. Realizing the importance of this fascination, the friars allowed native music and dancers clothed in brilliant plumes to participate in religious pageants and processions. The atrio was the ideal place to hold such manifestations.

On ordinary weekdays the atrio was used for religious and secular instruction; the Indian was taught to read and write, received religious education, was baptized, married and buried here.

The focal point of the atrio was a great stone or wooden cross placed in the center of the forecourt. There are no wooden crosses left, but the ones made of stone remain, displaying an inordinate originality and beauty. Father Motolinía wrote, in his *History of the Indians of New Spain (c. 1540):*

> *Everywhere in this land the emblem of the Cross is raised aloft. . . . It is said that in no part of the Christian world is the Cross found so often, esteemed so highly, adorned so richly, and made so large. Those in the patios of the churches are especially stately, and every Sunday and feast day the Indians adorn them with many roses, other flowers and garlands.*

Abstract symbols from the Passion of Christ were usually depicted in the carving of the crosses, Christian in spirit but with an interpretation definitely indigenous. The result was the tequitqui stylization, the Mexican counterpart to the Christian-Moorish mudéjar style, the crisp and vigorous result of European forms blending with non-European craftsmanship. It was primarily in these crosses that Indian creativity emerged in full force. In spite of the fact that the friars kept constant watch for any sign of pagan atavism on the part of their flock, and tried to check any visible impulse of idolatrous regression, the natives revered their crosses with a passionate possessiveness, regarding them as magic objects, like the idols they replaced, and believing them to carry the power of their fallen gods. The friars frequently found idols buried at the base of the cross, in Cholula, for example. Shortly after the Franciscans arrived there, they replaced a native shrine with a cross on the top of a pagan pyramid. Struck by lightning, the original cross was replaced, only to be struck again. When the friars dug deep holes to provide a strong foundation for the third cross they discovered a cache of idols and sea-snail trumpets. After destroying the idols and planting the last cross, there was no more lightning on that spot, a fact which no doubt made a strong impression on the Indians. Another story concerns the extraordinary reverence displayed by the natives towards the stone cross in Jilotepec. It was constantly decorated with garlands of flowers and the Indians kept a smoothly swept path in front of it. The friars were naturally pleased with this display of piety and decided to pave the area around it. The Indians protested but the friars went ahead with the project only to find a large number of idols buried beneath.

Similar crosses were also placed in cloistered patios and in public crossroads, but the most magnificent and dynamic are those found in the atrios.

The original purpose of the atrio became obsolete after about 1580. Several epidemics of smallpox and plague had decimated the Indian population; consequently there was enough room inside the churches to accommodate the survivors. Also enough generations had passed since the Conquest that the Indian no longer identified so strongly with his pagan past. Since he had no personal recollection of preconquest ritual, the psychological tie of the atrio and the teocalli was no longer pertinent.

The design of sixteenth-century atrios continued to persist in the seventeenth, although on a smaller scale. Even small posas were built, no longer free-standing but incorporated into the walls enclosing the new, smaller atrios.

There exist few examples of sixteenth-century atrios in metropolitan areas today. The few that do exist have been mutilated due to the urban growth which has engulfed them. Fortunately the friars' work extended to the countryside where the twentieth century has made little intrusion, thereby leaving the 400 year-old legacy unscathed.

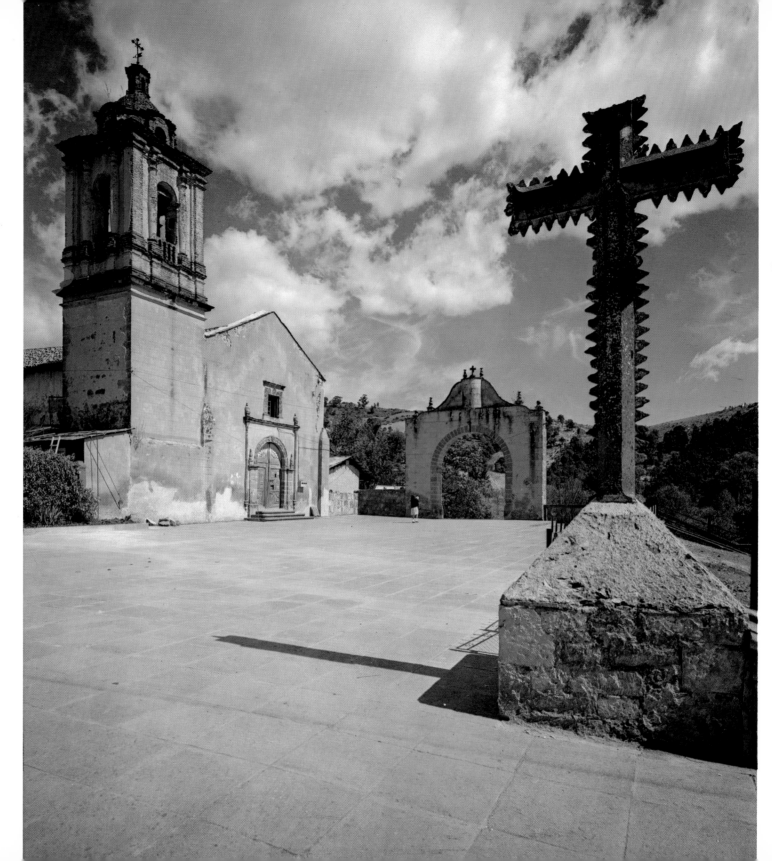

Photograph by Armando Salas Portugal

TLALPUJAHUA, MICHOACÁN.
Atrio and church, elevated from the surrounding village, dominate the rural townscape. Lacking in religious symbolism, the monolithic cross is a departure from the majority of atrio crosses, its serrated edge making a lively and dynamic silhouette.

89

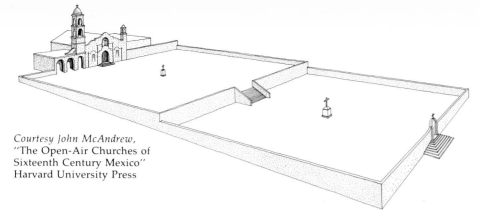

Overlooking the valley and lakes of Texcoco, the monastery complex occupies a Precolumbian religious center made up of three terraces. The two lower terraces were converted by the Franciscans into a double atrio, now heavily wooded by cypress and eucalyptus. The monastery building was built on the third and highest terrace, doubtless upon the site originally occupied by a teocalli.

HUEXOTLA, MEXICO

Photograph by Armando Salas Portugal

As many atrio crosses, this one is believed to have been carved from a Precolumbian idol—a plausible assumption since this would visibly manifest the transition from pagan to Christian belief. Another link between the old religion and the new is the Tequitqui ornamentation on the limbs of the cross—a hybrid between the Resurrection lily and native maize, symbol of the god Quetzalcoatl.

SANTA CRUZ ATOYAC. MÉXICO, D. F.

The 400 year-old olive which dominates the atrio is one of the few allowed to grow following the Conquest. The trees were strictly forbidden since its cultivation in Mexico posed a threat to the balance of trade with Spain.

SANTA CRUZ ATOYAC. MÉXICO, D. F.

Photograph by Armando Salas Portugal

VALLE DE LEOMA, MEXICO.

The original concept of the atrio is obsolete. No longer must a vast outdoor space be provided for a multitude of Indian converts. Yet, its surrounding walls continue to serve, shelter and function. Here it lies for Sunday's resurrection. In the interim this particular enclosed space serves a secular function as village drying yard for "tules" later to be fashioned into brooms.

The animistic beliefs to which the Indian converts adhered is evident in the carved relief of many atrio crosses. One of the most striking of these is at Acolman, whose representation of Veronica's veil is executed with dynamic directness. Symbols of the Passion are depicted along the shaft, and on the base the Virgin emerges with a cryptic resemblance to the goddess Tzintzuntzan.

Only on these crosses was native artistry given full reign, resulting in Tequitqui stylization—the combination of European concepts merging with the vitality of indigenous craftsmanship.

Courtesy I.N.A.H.

ACOLMAN, MEXICO

Photograph by Armando Salas Portugal

ATLACOMULCO, MEXICO.

Splendid in its starkness, trees and planting a long-forgotten feature, the atrio's architectonic beauty is exposed. Although visually fortress-like, the bristling crenels and merlons of the walls were decorative rather than defensive.

Photograph by Armando Salas Portugal

COACALCO, MEXICO.

Elevated from its surrounding village on the summit of a hill, church and atrio are the landmark of the region. The mantle of greenery reinforces serenity within the wall, beckoning the villagers to share its peace.

95

CUAUTINCHÁN, PUEBLA.

The ascetic, timeless quality of this Franciscan atrio is emphasized by the bareness of its open spaces. The plantings which once flourished have long died. Windswept loneliness prevails. Only echoes of former glory remain. Walls— sentinels of the past—salute each other.

HUEJOTZINGO, PUEBLA.

Established in 1524 by Franciscans, the monastery was one of the first four in Mexico. All of its elements—convent, cloister, atrio and especially posas—are a tribute to the extraordinary combination of European and native skill. Along the side of the walls, a corridor of cobblestone leads from one posa to the next. The four posas, built by the middle of the century, are perhaps the most fascinating in the country. Seventeen feet on a side, all four are identical, with sculptured angles, each carrying a different instrument of the Passion, fitting naturally into the spandrels of the facade. As John McAndrew puts it, in the *Open-Air Churches of Sixteenth-Century Mexico*, "One easily imagines the teaching friars walking their pupils around the atrio, telling the story of the Passion, and explaining its significance, while pointing out the different carvings which illustrate, symbolize, and commemorate it."

Photograph by Armando Salas Portugal

AMECAMECA, MEXICO.

The atrio of many monastery complexes, as in this Dominican example, frequently faced the plaza of the village, thus providing a double-purpose expanse of greenery. A gateway of triumphal-arch proportions generally linked the secular world to the religious.

PATIOS

*Today ... our architecture has passed from the cave
to the garden, from the monument to the dwelling house.
But in throwing open our buildings to the daylight and
the outdoors, we will forget, at our peril, the coordinate
... need for quiet, for inner privacy, for retreat.*

— Lewis Mumford

Photograph by Armando Salas Portugal

QUADRANGLE OF THE NUNS. UXMAL, YUCATÁN

The vast Mayan courtyard corresponds in configuration and purpose to the traditional patio, differing only in proportion. Cells, housing priests and sanctuaries, enclose the Prehispanic cloister built six hundred years before Cortés.

THE ENCLOSED COURTYARD, or patio, was by no means a novel idea of the Mexican—indeed, the concept of a garden located within the confines of a building is virtually universal. Nebuchadnezzar's Babylon, Pliny's Pompeii, and Moctezuma's Tenochtitlán had similar variations of the patio concept: a natural sanctuary enclosed within the interior of a dwelling place. The Mexican patio as we know it today, however, has its roots in Spain.

After the Conquest, settlers from Spain joined the Conquerors in Mexico, bringing with them the image of the Spanish-Moorish patio. Affording absolute privacy and intimacy, it was the archetype of the outdoor room. Within a few years, homes and monasteries, all containing patios, burgeoned throughout the valleys. Anxious that Mexico be settled as quickly as possible, the Crown established the feudal system of the encomienda in which the settlers were awarded large grants of land and native labor. The newcomers were thus guaranteed a prosperous livelihood and a life of luxury and ease.

In the first decades after the Conquest, however, function and defense rather than aesthetics dictated the design of buildings. Fear of Indian attack produced structures which were relatively plain, broad, and strong; their silhouettes punctuated by battlements and merlons, causing Cervantes de Salazar, first rector of the University to exclaim, "One would say these were not houses but veritable fortresses!" This fear, however proved essentially unfounded. With few scattered exceptions, the Indian did not rebel but accepted his serfdom with amazing passivity. Doubtless his new freedom from active participation in the grisly Aztec sacrificial rites was a welcome relief.

The Viceregal period of Mexico spanned three hundred years. During this long reign Spain dictated not only policy but art and design as well. In these three centuries Spain and the Colonists reaped wealth and power at the expense of the subjugated Indian. With a seemingly inexhaustible supply of land and labor, magnificent homes, convents, haciendas, gardens, and churches were constructed.

The undisputably eclectic Spaniards brought with them the heritage of the Romans, Visigoths, and Moors. Aztec tradition of massive volumes and uncluttered planes gave way to the richness of the Romanesque, Gothic, and Mudéjar. Native artisans and craftsmen, whose skill was the result of generations of superb builders, responded to European building techniques and design with remarkable facility and speed.

Peace and prosperity marked the colonists's way of life and were reflected in his surroundings. Fortunes produced from silver mining, sugar plantations, and trade with the Orient resulted in sumptuous and exuberant environmental design. The Romanesque and Gothic of the sixteenth century evolved into seventeenth century Baroque and later, the Churrigueresque.

Throughout these periods of stylistic transformation, however, the basic design of the patio remained unchanged. Quadrangular in shape and surrounded by a covered arcaded corridor which opened into the various rooms of the house, the patio continued to be the nucleus of the building.

Since most of the rooms faced the patio, air and sunlight were introduced, as well as the view of its shrubbery, trees, and fountain.

Generally located in the center of the patio, the

ACOLMAN, MEXICO.

Photograph by Armando Salas Portugal

Privacy and serenity, the basis of monastic patios of the sixteenth century, are singularly evident in the cloister at Acolman. Built by the Augustinians, who, compared to the other Mendicant orders, tended to use a richer treatment of ornamental detailing, the four hundred year old patio retains a quality of unblemished elegance.

fountain was typically of Mudéjar design, a definite carryover from Iberian-Moorish tradition. Assuming several shapes, rectangular, hexagonal, or octagonal, it was usually placed in a stepped base which repeated the shape of the fountain. Potted plants were placed on the brim, a device which was not only colorful but practical. To water the plants, one simply scooped water from the fountain.

Tile abounded in the patio, providing bright accents of color throughout the courtyard. This came about with the immigration of Spanish tile-makers from Talavera who brought with them their exquisite craft of handpainted glazed tile. They settled in the town of Puebla, north of Mexico City, and soon the fruit of their artistry flourished throughout the country—in the domes of churches, facades of buildings, but most vividly in the benches and fountains of Mexican patios.

The paving of the patios was fashioned with cobbles, adobe, or handcut stone. Intricate mosaics of varicolored stone were frequently designed into the paving, a time-consuming and laborious job, but one at which the Indian builders were masters. The paved areas led to the center of the patio, with beds of planting between them.

Although Mexican patios were a direct copy of those found in Andalucía, they assumed a freshness and spontaneity quite different from their Spanish prototypes. Introduced into Spain by the Moors, the patio originated in a land of intense light and heat. Contained and shaded by the surrounding building, the patios of Andalucía offered a welcome respite from the glare of the scorching sun and dust of the arid terrain—a refreshing oasis in a bleak and baked environment. Intimate and cool, the patio was the soul of the Spanish home.

In Mexico, the function of the patio remained the same as in Spain—a haven of privacy and peace. Its physical aspect, however, in relation to size and treatment, was subtly transformed. The patios of Spain, notably those in the Alcazar and the Alhambra, were built on a grand scale, extraordinary in their Moorish detailing and extensive mirrors of water. But these were exceptions constructed for potentates within a palatial setting. The popular patios which abounded in Seville and Granada were comparatively modest in configuration and size. In Mexico, the ample availability of space produced homes and buildings larger than those across the ocean; their courtyard gardens more generous and spacious.

The gentle subtropic climate of central Mexico was also a vivid departure from the aridity of Spain. The Mexican patio was not a retreat from the sun, but a place to revel in its benign rays. The climate produced an incredible variety of native plants, adding a dimension which was unknown in Castile. At that time, bougainvillaea, so frequently associated with Spanish patios had not been introduced to Europe from Brazil, and the plant palette of Spain tended to be somber and muted. The dark greens and grays of myrtle and olive, the formality of cedar and cypress were supplanted in Mexico by purple jacaranda and blood-orange poincianna, by exuberant frangipani and morning-glory trees, infusing the patios with brilliant color and exotic form.

Thus the configuration of the model, with its basic components of plants reflecting upon a water-brimming pool, was retained; but the dimension of the offspring was greater, its hues brighter, more intense and unrestrained.

Courtesy Artes de México

RESIDENTIAL PATIO. MÉXICO, D. F.

103

CHURUBUSCO, MÉXICO, D. F.

The conventual garden of Churubusco follows the Spanish-Moorish tradition of using glazed tiles to add color to an otherwise green garden. The Mudéjar octagonal fountain and benches recall their counterparts in the patios of Seville.

CHURUBUSCO CONVENT, MÉXICO, D. F.

Massive columns and arches supporting the upper story convey a contrapuntal essay of repeated harmonies. The architectonic inner cloister of this seventeenth-century convent appears majestically austere compared to the gaily tiled orchard patio. As often was the case, the conventual complexes contained several patios, linking the various wings of the buildings.

HUEJOTZINGO, PUEBLA.

The fountain of the early conventual patios assumed various forms—circular, octagonal, hexagonal, with or without platforms. Here an octagonal fountain varies with the addition of extended spoke-like members; an innovation and the only one quite like it. The patio, as well as the rest of this Franciscan convent, has been allowed to deteriorate, a pity since its atrio and extraordinary posas, together with the original cloister, are remarkable in age and beauty.

105

TEPOZTLÁN, MÉXICO.

The pool of the service patio is a reservoir from a nearby aqueduct within this Jesuit monastery. Despite the humble, utilitarian function, native builders produced a masterful composition of light and shade, stone and water.

PATIO DE LAS NARANJAS
TEPOZTLÁN, MÉXICO.

Orange trees, for which the patio is named, comprise the only planting within this sixteenth-century cloister. This, with the use of cobblestone paving, results in a courtyard that requires little maintenance. The straightforward design and restraint of materials have allowed this patio to appear unchanged since its construction.

COLEGIO DE LAS VISCAÍNAS. MÉXICO, D. F.

Photograph by Armando Salas Portugal

Built on a grand scale, the distinctive patio is typical of the great civic courtyards of the seventeenth and eighteenth centuries. Surrounded by one of the most notable structures of its epoch, the patio articulates the spaciousness of such Mexican enclosures. The school originally was commissioned by a group of philanthropic Spaniards from Biscay to give impoverished and underprivileged girls an educational opportunity.

The architectonic patio is elegantly austere, its rich, ornamental detailing of the fountain, arches, and spandrels exemplifying its baroque character.

PALACIO FEDERAL, QUERÉTARO, QUERÉTARO.

The arches of the mirador surround the central patio of this hacienda. Although the patio is devoid of planting, the myriad of tiles in the gateway, the fountain platform, and the arcade infuse the patio with color. Stone frogs spit water into the pool, a device frequently used.

HACIENDA LA GAVIA, MÉXICO.

One of the earliest homes to be built after the Conquest, the house originally belonged to one of Cortés' lieutenants, Diego de Ordaz. Simple square columns contrast with the brilliant sheen of the glazed tile planters.

108

CASA DE DIEGO DE ORDAZ, MÉXICO, D. F.

Tassels and masks of molded plaster (yesería) accentuate the low wall surrounding this eighteenth-century patio. The reddish rust of the balustrade, pool, and paving supplies the garden with color, dispensing with the need for flowers. The house came under the protection of the National Institute of History and became the museum of equestrian art, "El Museo de la Charrería."

CASA CHATA, MÉXICO, D. F.

109

CASA LANZAGORTA. SAN MIGUEL ALLENDE, GUANAJUATO.

A filigree of wrought iron, not colonial but Porfirian, named after the great eclectic, President Porfirio Díaz, divides the roofed entry from the open-air patio. The neo-Classic double-tiered fountain, elegantly sumptuous, splashes water into the acanthus-carved stone fountain. By the eighteenth century, the simple Andalucían-inspired patio had evolved into an outdoor room of aristocratic, and ultra-baroque design.

110

Particularly suited for the tropical climate of Veracruz, the patio becomes a cool green haven from the midday heat, its *corredor* a refuge from the rain. Here a modest patio, its pillars without arches or capitals, looks onto a virtual jungle.

RESIDENTIAL PATIO. TLACOTALPAN, VERACRUZ.

Photograph by Armando Salas Portugal

PRIVATE RESIDENCE, PUEBLA, PUEBLA.

A baroque zaghuán, or entryway, opens
into the eighteenth-century patio. Characteristic of the patios of Puebla, home of
Talavera tile , the intimate courtyard focuses on a wall-fountain totally encrusted
with brilliant profusion of tile.

The Casa Requena represents Mexican adaptation of the Art Nouveau movement which swept Europe in the late nineteenth century. In the patio, glazed tile was not only abundant, it was redundant: natural plants and birds did not suffice but were repeated in the tiles.

CASA REQUENA, MÉXICO, D. F.

Within the last four decades, modern architecture emerged in Mexico, the force of its impact sweeping the country. Nostalgia for Colonial architecture persists, however, and with it, affection for the traditional patio. This affinity with the past led to the restoration of decaying historical haciendas and homes many of which have been converted into resorts and restaurants. Here rhythmical arches illuminated from within dramatize a stately fountain. Resurrected by Belloli, the patio of a long-abandoned silver mill evokes an incandescent memory of grandeur.

GIORGIO BELLOLI: HACIENDA SANTA ANNA, MARFIL, GUANAJUATO.

HACIENDA LA GOICOCHEA, MÉXICO, D. F.

In the early 1970s, all that remained of the eighteenth-century country estate was its nucleus of structures and adjacent patios, its lush surrounding acreage sacrificed to suburbanization. The historic hacienda, site of political intrigue and drama during the turbulent years of the Revolution, had since been converted into one of the most elegant restaurants of Mexico City; San Angel Inn. The open masonry or citarilla wall along the upper corridor overlooks the quiet patio. The hand-carved sculptured fountain retains the presence of the hand of man.

113

Photograph by Armando Salas Portugal

HACIENDA LOS MORALES, MÉXICO.

The splash of an eighteenth-century fountain fills the sunlit patio with a rejoicing murmur—a welcome sound midst the cacophonous twentieth century. Traditional geranium pots girdle the fountain step, bringing vivid color with a minimum of maintenance.

A half-opened portal opens into the zaghuán, allowing
a streetside glimpse into the patio beyond. Conforming
to traditional design of Colonial patios, the arcaded
corridor links the interior of the home with the garden.
Unabashed indigo of walls reverberates throughout—a
season hence orange poincianna will vie for attention.

PRIVATE RESIDENCE, ALAMOS, SONORA.

GARDENS OF SECLUSION

Thus we seek two values in every landscape:
one, the expression ot the native quality
of the landscape, the other,
the development of maximum human livability.

—Garrett Eckbo

ABOVE ANY OTHER, the design of the private garden is carried on with a maximum freedom. The materials from which gardens are made—earth, water, stone, plants—are incomparable in their natural state. They beckon to follow suit—but do not command. Man makes his choice to transform or manipulate, to enhance or mutilate these natural instruments—or simply to leave them alone. The beauty lies in the fact that the choice is his.

The private garden is therefore a personal thing. In the course of its development, it has elicited its maker to relish the feel of his own soil, to breathe the fragrance of a flower planted by his own choice. Thus the garden expresses a definite statement of its owner, one which is frequently intuitive and thoroughly subjective, allowing him to satisfy his personal taste and needs.

The need for solitude is best answered in the quiet of a secluded garden. It offers a retreat from the world outside, a private haven from whatever pressures are encountered in the daily business of living. Whatever is within the garden wall is not for public perusal, but remains the private concern and delight of its owner.

In Mexico such garden walls are emphatically stated—relatively free from archaic zoning codes and ordinances—a positive assertion bearing no self-conscious apology for undemocratic seclusion.

These insure the privilege to seek solace and peace, to sit or walk among hushed greenery without fear of intrusion. This is a personal place, offering that most personal of freedoms, privacy. The concept of the patio—so fundamental an element in Mexican landscape architecture—retains its significance in contemporary gardens. Although no longer a central courtyard surrounded by the building, the garden retains a feeling of enclosure.

Walls are the structural backbone of the modern patio, and it is the placement, treatment, and proportion of these which set contemporary Mexican patios apart from traditional ones. When left unencumbered from their familiar tapestry of vines, these planes become singular statements in themselves.

Nor is there timidity in the use of color. Not here the neutral shades favored by Americans, to whom brilliant pigment sometimes bears the stigma of "bad taste." Unselfconscious and spontaneous, these vivid planes echo the spectacle of brilliant vegetation in which Mexico abounds.

Contemporary gardens of Mexico possess an underlying quality which is singularly unmistakable. The fabric of past centuries is tenacious; the twentieth century result is architectonically bold and vividly unforgettable.

Photograph by Armando Salas Portugal

Andrés Casillas: Residential Patio. México, D. F.

119

This residential courtyard exemplifies the Mexican proclivity for undisturbed planes. Interrelated textures—wood, stone, water and concrete—provide the elements of interest and contrast.

JUAN SORDO MADALENO: PRIVATE RESIDENCE, MÉXICO, D. F.

Free-standing walls are left bare except for the contemporary crucifix by Mathías Goeritz. The walls are a pristine background for the ever-changing play of shadows cast by the sculpture. The sharp angularity of the container-grown yucca adds to the stark drama of the garden. The restraint of this contemporary patio emphasizes the natural tangle of the eucalyptus grove beyond.

GIORGIO BELLOLI: PRIVATE RESIDENCE, MARFIL, GUANAJUATO.

The long slender pool is terraced within the improbable topography of the Guanajuato region. Fitting into the Colonial setting of a centuries-old aqueduct, the garden exemplifies that remarkable facet of Mexican environmental design—a carefree and harmonious juxtaposition of past and present.

MARIO OGURI: PRIVATE RESIDENCE, CUERNAVACA, MORELOS.

Panels of glass overlook a continuous garden corridor which wraps around the house. The unrestrained vegetation of the garden belies its limited width; each room is expanded to include the outdoors.

The miniscule, atrium-like patio divides dining from living room. The Colonial planter, used as a fountain, introduces an accent from another era with a delightful degree of success. The beauty of the tiny garden lies in the rich combination of plant materials—fragrant plumeria, scarlet blossomed glory bush, and feathery pigmy date palm.

MARIO OGURI: CUERNAVACA, MORELOS.

Photograph by Armando Salas Portugal

In keeping with the feeling of the garden as an outdoor room, the contemporary patio is contained and easy to maintain. A facsimile of an Aztec jaguar, its prototype used in pre-Colonial times as a depository of sacrificed hearts, becomes the focal point.

PEDRO RAMÍREZ VÁSQUEZ: OFFICE ENTRANCE, MÉXICO, D. F.

Hovering over a brimming mirror of water, the replica of a pre-Colonial head complements the contemporary lines of the building. Behind the grill the branches of a coral tree cast their reflection, uniting private and public space.

PEDRO RAMÍREZ VÁSQUEZ: RESIDENTIAL PATIO, MÉXICO, D. F.

124

Juan O'Gorman:
Private Residence, México, D. F.

The implementation of mosaic, notable among O'Gorman's many talents, is used as a tool to link structure and surrounding nature. The multi-colored stones leading from the serpent-like parapet through the facade of the house to the pattern of the paving, neutralize the demarkation between man and nature — structure becomes an integral part of natural surroundings.

A cross in relief emerges from a patio wall, its ever-changing shadow adds a kinetic quality to an otherwise static plane. Opposite the cross, a trough-like pool is used by the nuns to arrange flowers for the nearby altar. A minute spillway channels the overflow onto the reservoir below, a time-worn device used by the Persians. The dark finish of the pool, constantly filled to the brim, produces a mirror-image of the modular concrete screen. The designer responded to the austerity of the cloistered life—the restraint and simplicity of the patio reflects the life-style of the Capuchin nuns for whom it was designed.

LUIS BARRAGÁN: CONVENTUAL PATIO, TLALPAM, D. F.

LUIS BARRAGÁN: CONVENTUAL PATIO, TLALPAM, D. F.

Adjoining the chapel of the convent the tranquil garden recalls the monastery patios of the sixteenth century. The components are the same, water, plants and enclosing walls—only their arrangement and design mark the passing of four hundred years.

127

The natural quality of the garden extends to the weathered twisting form of the dead branch, which, in the role of sculpture, provides a vertical accent dramatically dominating the esplanade of lawn.

Luis Barragán: Residential Garden, México, D. F.

Stone steps, terraces and retaining walls wrap around an unobtrusive pool in a series of bold and simple planes. Twisting branches of pepper trees entwine above lush acanthus, giving this all-natural garden a timeless, almost primordial quality.

Photograph by Armando Salas Portugal

LUIS BARRAGÁN: PRIVATE RESIDENCE, MÉXICO, D. F.

Photograph by Armando Salas Portugal

The ultimate tools of the landscape architect are the raw materials of nature—earth, water, and living plants under a dome of infinite sky. In this garden each material fuses with its neighbor yet retains its own character. Coral trees spring from a bed of lava which encroaches upon the pool of water. The water in turn completes the cycle by reflecting the trees and sky above.

Photograph by Armando Salas Portugal

The coral tree, *(Erythrina americana)* is as integral a component of the Pedregal as the swirls of black lava. For generations the tree was ignored, allowed to grow wild in its native habitat, its remarkable potential as a major design element unrecognized. The discovery that a full-grown tree such as this one could survive the shock of transplant, even with extensive root damage, was a boon for landscape architects. Its endurance and its structural beauty, lime-green foliage, and crimson-spiked blossoms converted it into one of the common denominators of the Pedregal.

LUIS BARRAGÁN: PRIVATE RESIDENCE,

PEDREGAL GARDENS, MÉXICO, D. F.

131

Photograph by Armando Salas Portugal

LUIS BARRAGÁN: PRIVATE RESIDENCE, LAS ARBOLEDAS, MÉXICO

Unencumbered planes of vibrant color and proportion dominate the great courtyard adjoining a stable of thoroughbreds. Riders, coming from the surrounding pasture, enter through the double gateway to a broad shallow pool in the center of the enclosure. Jutting into the pool a great aqueduct spills a torrent of water out of the trough-like sluice. Narrow stone shingles pave the area, gradually sloping towards the water's edge and slipping into the pool. A detail of the garden appears on the jacket of this book.

THREE

EVERYMAN'S LANDSCAPE

In spite of technological progress, or perhaps because of its spottiness,
our man-made environment has shown an ominous tendency to slip more and more
out of control. The farther man has moved away from the balanced integration of nature,
the more his physical environment has become harmful.

— *Richard Neutra*

THE OPEN SPACES in the midst of the city are a mirror of man within it. The image of his beliefs, attitudes, and values is reflected by the nature and quality of his physical surroundings. A depressed community is instantly and intensely perceived by the neglect and disregard of its outdoor spaces: dessicated tree, windblown earth, and waterless fountain tell the story — survival is the prime concern. Conversely, verdant park, cleanswept square, and treelined street echo a healthy, vigorous society.

Embracing and threading through the urban landscape, these areas are the common bond, the link, between the city's extremes. As town square, park, or empty lot, they occupy a major position within the hierarchy of the urban whole, providing the landscape character of a given place. The best of these, the sensitively and thoughtfully designed plazas, parks, and streets, subtly unify and reinforce the structures which surround them. In the scheme of man-made environment, the essence of the place is in effect distilled by the presence and quality of the open space which surrounds it.

Nor do these areas assume a passive role within the city's drama. Human activity is indeed reinforced by the dimension and design of the physical setting which envelops it.

This interaction between man and his physical environment makes the urban landscape a kinetic and dynamic entity. As his life-style, habits, and tra-ditions change, so does the character of his public open space — everyman's landscape.

This man-land relationship is remarkably vivid in the central highlands of Mexico, specifically in the vicinities near the nation's capital.

The Valley has changed. Six hundred years of evolution and growth have led to the Mexico of today. The transformation from the chinampas surrounded by lake water to a twentieth-century megalopolis of more than ten million inhabitants was inevitable. The capital, so long the heart from which culture, science, and progress flowed, continues to be a magnet, drawing industry, commerce, and art from the rest of the Republic. Mexico City teems with life and bristles with vitality — and faces the same problems that plague all major urban centers: congestion, slums, traffic, and smog. Worldwide homogeneity, that ever-pervasive course upon which all civilization seems directed, has not bypassed the ancient Vale of Anáhuac. Outlying villages now share the same Coca Cola signs of outlying villages everywhere.

Yet there exists an undercurrent of individuality and self-identity which resists the blanket of universal sameness and exerts itself in specific areas of the physical environment. This impetus is expressed in certain outstanding examples of contemporary environmental design in which aesthetic and spiritual concerns often transcend those of function and finance. It is this variant of emphasis, perhaps, which lends the quality of uniqueness to Mexican landscape architecture. Just as the gardens of Japan are imbued with a distinct identity, the outstanding gardens and open spaces of modern Mexico similarly possess a corresponding distinction.

Referring to what he describes as the native "accent" found in contemporary Mexican design, José Villagrán García, Mexico's foremost professor of architecture, writes, "The Mexican usage of the tri-dimensional sense of space can be discerned in much of our present work, in tactile surfaces but more especially in habitable spaces, patios, corridors, terraces, walks and courtyards. The play of depth and light embodies but does not coincide with that achieved in the remote past." This intuitive sense of scale and proportion, whose roots reach to the Precolumbian past, has been a constant element throughout Mexico's history, manifested today in a constant dynamism and generosity of volumes and open spaces. There remains a conscious effort to integrate the essence of the natural with that which is man-made, considering the value of open spaces on a par with structure.

A recurring element contributing to this regional characteristic is the freedom with which color, light, and texture are implemented. An unembarrassed spontaneity is expressed in the interplay and combination of contrasting hues and tactile surface treatment.

This quality, the native "accent," which prevails throughout the contemporary landscape, could not exist but for the presence of a natural constant, the benign climatic and ecological condition of the Valley of Mexico. Since man first tilled its soil, Mexico has given fruit to all manner of green growing things, producing what is probably the most abundant and varied flora in the world. This vast array — more than 20,000 different species of plants, — has been nature's special contribution.

Yet of these constants, the quality of labor produced by the Mexican himself is the noblest of all. From the fabrication of the garden chinampas of Tenochtitlán, through the Tequitqui manifestation of sixteenth-century atrio crosses, to the hand-hewn bas-relief retaining walls of the University City, the imprint of human craftmanship, the "mano de obra," has signally lent itself to the essence of Mexico's physical environment.

Irrefutably, contemporary Mexican design is a subtle distillation of its history. Yet, in its application to modern problems, it transcends any suggestion of eclecticism, emerging instead as a force that is stunningly original.

Whatever its heritage, the shaping of Mexico's urban landscape is a tapestry of dynamic shapes and vibrant hues. The outcome is a place whose landscape character is vivid, often startling — but above all — Mexican.

PROMETHEUS FOUNTAIN, UNIVERSITY CITY, MÉXICO, D. F.
Rodrigo Betancourt, sculptor.

Perhaps no other site in Mexico articulates contemporary environmental design as vividly as University City. Located in the Pedregal, in the southern fringe of Mexico City, it replaced the venerable University of Mexico, the oldest in the Americas, founded in 1551. One hundred fifty environmental designers, sculptors, architects, landscape architects, and urban planners rallied to bring the work to completion in three years. Respecting the irregular topography of the lava field, the site planners happily departed from a rigid spatial organization, responding directly to the rugged quality of the terrain.

The open spaces of the campus expose, complement, and reinforce the spectacular architecture of the University. Paving of pebble-studded concrete connects the Humanities building (foreground), Library, and Rectory. Humanizing the immense scale of the campus, unexpected groves of pepper trees relieve the huge expanses. Intimate pockets of greenery are as conscientiously designed as the structures which surround them.

UNIVERSITY CITY, MÉXICO, D. F.

Photograph by Armando Salas Portugal

ALBERTO ARAI: FRONTÓN COURTS,
UNIVERSITY CITY, MÉXICO, D. F.

The game of frontón, its roots in the time before the Conquest, is similar to tennis and handball. The courts are enclosed on three sides by high smooth walls upon which the ball is bounced. The truncated pyramidal shape of the courts is a conscious acknowledgment of Mexico's Prehispanic heritage —yet the slope of the outer wall is functional as well, allowing sufficient space for dressing rooms and showers between the walls. Aside from their Prehispanic evocation, the inclined planes of volcanic stone echo the surrounding landscape which in itself consists of lava outcrops of similar configuration.

139

The driveway and entrance of this hotel are spectacular in their elegant simplicity. The lobby faces a huge basin of ever-turbulent water set in an expanse of white marble. Strategically located underwater jets produce the churning waves—perhaps a preparation for the onrush of traffic beyond. The free-standing Goeritz screen adds to the richness of the place by the hypnotic juxtaposition of positive and negative shapes.

Ricardo Legorreta, Architect; Mathías Goeritz, Sculptor.

Hotel Camino Real, México, D. F.

140

142   Courtesy Clive B. Smith, *Builders in the Sun*,
© 1967, Architectural Book Publishing Co.

MANUEL DE LA ROSA, ARCHITECTS; FELIX CANDELA, CONSULTANT:
OPEN CHAPEL, LOMAS DE CUERNAVACA, MORELOS. GUILLERMO ROSSELL,

The wide mouth of the hyperbolic-parabaloid concrete
chapel is planted with a grove of royal poinciannas which
shade the pews beneath. This marriage of structure and
landscape is a masterful and dynamic evocation of the
sixteenth-century open chapel, atrio and cross.

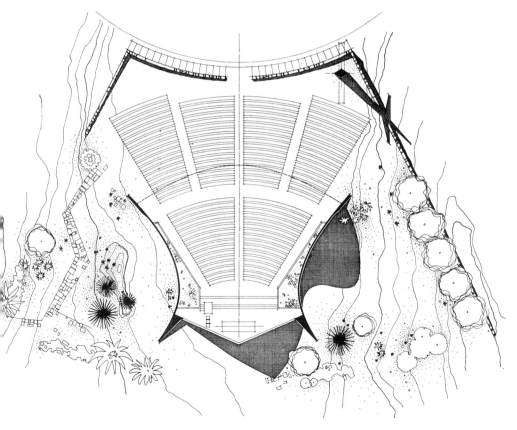

Photograph by Armando Salas Portugal

Courtesy Clive B. Smith, *Builders in the Sun*, © 1967, *Architectural Book Publishing Co.*

144

RICARDO LEGORRETA, ARCHITECT; MATHIAS GOERITZ, SCULPTOR:
FORECOURT, AUTOMEX FACTORY, HIGHWAY TO TOLUCA, MÉXICO.

The generosity of space and materials in conjunction with bold and uncluttered design—always a dominant feature in the landscape architecture of Mexico—is apparent in the entrance of this automobile assembly plant. Goeritz's concrete towers, 35 feet high, loom over the surrounding countryside, an example of what he refers to as "environmental sculpture."

LUIS BARRAGÁN:
STREET INTERSECTION, LAS ARBOLEDAS, MÉXICO.

The most visible component in the urban environment is the
street, its treatment becoming a major stimulus, retained in
the memory of those who view it. In this street intersection,
inclined planes of stucco and brick come into balance, visually
resolving the irregular topography.

Photograph by Armando Salas Portugal

Photograph by Armando Salas Portugal

LUIS BARRAGÁN, IN COLLABORATION WITH MATHÍAS GOERITZ:
TOWERS OF THE SATÉLITE SUBDIVISION, MÉXICO, D. F.

These improbable concrete towers, the tallest
soaring 164 feet into the sky, were conceived
as a landmark for Ciudad Satélite, one of
Mexico's first planned communities. Located
in the median of a major highway leading into
Mexico City, the slender landmarks are visible
for miles. Color, form and scale coalesce to
produce visual impact of impressive magnitude
relieving the grey monotony of asphalt and steel.

Photograph by Armando Salas Portugal

Frozen in a sea of lava, the volcanic terrain of the Pedregal stood barren and isolated from the rest of Mexico City. The area lay dormant, shunned by land developers because of its forbidding topography and save for a few scattered shacks, abandoned. Fascinated by the plutonic landscape, Barragán envisioned its transformation from a no-man's land to urban dwellings. His approach was to retain the remarkable character of the lava flows and incorporate these with contemporary architecture, maintaining and complementing the beauty and integrity of each.

LUIS BARRAGÁN: PEDREGAL GARDENS SUBDIVISION, MÉXICO, D. F.

Photograph by Armando Salas Portugal

LUIS BARRAGÁN: PEDREGAL GARDENS, MÉXICO, D. F.

Water stops at the edge of the brimful pool, without interruption between it and the landscape beyond. Barragán's statements in stone and water are singular in their simplicity —they do not vie with the natural but enhance and reinforce it. The result is a rare dialogue between the natural and the man-made.

147

Marking the entrance to the Pedregal Gardens, the serpent sculpture evokes the coatepantli surrounding the temple precinct of pre-Hispanic Tenochtitlán which in its time similarly heralded the entrance to a unique site.

LUIS BARRAGÁN: PEDREGAL GARDENS, MÉXICO, D. F.

Slender steel posts, often devoid of horizontal members, thread throughout the subdivision, becoming as characteristic of the Pedregal as the ubiquitous coral tree and the purple-black lava. Simplicity and restraint are demanded by the tumultuous landscape; superfluous ornamentation would disrupt the drama supplied by nature.

Photograph by Armando Salas Portugal

149

LUIS BARRAGÁN: PLAZA DEL
CAMPANARIO, LAS ARBOLEDAS,
MÉXICO.

Barragán approached the planning of Las Arboledas in the
same manner as he did the virgin landscape of the Pedregal,
retaining the natural character
of the terrain as much as possible. The introduction of water
intensifies the natural quality
of the site—nature is manipu-
lated with superb mastery.

150

Photograph by Armando Salas Portugal

LUIS BARRAGÁN: PLAZA DEL
BEBEDERO DE LOS CABALLOS,
LAS ARBOLEDAS, MÉXICO.

The forested subdivision contains a series of bridle paths
which meander throughout the
area. Riders coming in from the
surrounding woods stop to
water their horses at the brimming trough. The design of this
equestrian plaza is superbly
simple; the result, however, is
kinetic in the glimmering
reflection of the pool and chang-
ing shadows cast on the wall
by the eucalyptus trees.

Photograph by Armando Salas Portugal

151

LUIS BARRAGÁN: LOS CLUBES, LAS ARBOLEDAS, MÉXICO.

The water garden, one of several in the equestrian oriented subdivision, is an abstraction of vertical and horizontal planes, with the single gush of water reinforcing the simplicity of the setting. Derelict horse troughs entitled *Los Amantes* — the lovers — are utilized as sculpture. Dark, smooth cobblestones lead and blend into the water, its mirror-like surface adding the quality of reflection. Pool and fountain were conceived as a watering place for horses — thus the superhuman scale.

152

LUIS BARRAGÁN: LOS CLUBES, LAS ARBOLEDAS, MÉXICO.

153

MARIO PANI: NONOALCO-TLATELOLCO HOUSING DEVELOPMENT, MÉXICO, D. F.

At opposite extremes from the affluent serenity of the Pedregal and Las Arboledas, the urban renewal project was created to replace a major ghetto in the heart of Mexico City. Its towering skyscrapers have been deprecated by some as being "inhumane"—the fact remains that the housing complex released 70,000 inhabitants from a life of overcrowded squalor. Alleviating the harshness of surrounding concrete and steel, Nonoalco-Tlateloloco—a city within a city—devotes more than 50 percent of its total area to green spaces such as this children's park.

An affinity between the new and the old is
one of the remarkable aspects of the Mexican
urbanscape. A sixteenth-century cross coexists
in harmony with the twentienth-century building. Although four centuries separate the two,
they are comfortable in each other's presence.

MARIO PANI: NONOALCO-TLATELOLCO
HOUSING DEVELOPMENT, MÉXICO, D. F.

Photograph by Armando Salas Portugal

Courtesy Clive B. Smith, *Builders in the Sun*,
© 1967, *Architectural Book Publishing Co.*

PEDRO RAMÍREZ VÁSQUEZ: NATIONAL MUSEUM OF ANTHROPOLOGY, MÉXICO, D. F.

Housing what is virtually the world's richest collection of archaeological treasures, the eleven-acre site nestles in the midst of Chapultepec Park; an apt setting since it was here that the people who embodied the culmination of Prehispanic Mexico—the Aztecs—first settled in 1325. An immense forecourt leads to the entrance of the museum, providing a welcome rest area for visitors. A bower of trees shades the occasional seats of hand-hewn stone, subtly carved for human comfort.

156

Photograph by Armando Salas Portugal

Clean-swept volumes and planes mark the essence of Mexico's anthropological museum. A single tree binds the cantilevered aluminum overhang with the hand-carved cantera stone. Cut and fitted by hand, the cantera is evidence of Mexico's long suit, the "mano de obra" — hand-labor — which is manifest everywhere.

PEDRO RAMÍREZ VÁSQUEZ: CENTRAL PATIO, NATIONAL MUSEUM OF ANTHROPOLOGY, MÉXICO, D. F.

Surrounded by archaeological treasures of Mexico's past, the 600-foot-long patio is a vivid representation of the present. The umbrella-like overhang of suspended aluminum thrusts out from the top of a 40-foot-high stone shaft. Encircling the shaft, a sheet of water cascades onto the black cantera paving. Small holes collect the recirculated water. The imposing courtyard, like the archaeological artifacts beyond, celebrates the tenacity of man's artistic presence on earth.

Photograph by Armando Salas Portugal

Pedro Ramírez Vásquez: Museum of Anthropology, México, D. F.

A serene pool reflects and complements the tension of the canopy. A stylized conch, Indian symbol of wind, faces the lagoon. Designed to carry the park-like feeling into the building, inmense glass walls and doors open onto the surrounding gardens and forest of Chapultepec. This blending of indoor and outdoor space, together with the conjunction of past and present, results in a site unrivaled in its integration of space and time.

SOURCES

Baird, Joseph Armstrong Jr. *The Churches of Mexico 1530-1810*. Los Angeles: University of California Press, 1962.

Benítez, Fernando. *Los Primeros Mexicanos; la vida criolla en el siglo XVI*. México: Ediciones Erg, 1962.

Bernal, Ignacio. *Tenochtitlán en una isla*. México: I.N.A.H., 1959.

————.*Mexico Before Cortés: Art, History and Legend*. Translated of above title by Willes Barnstone, Garden City, N.Y.: Dolphin Books; Doubleday & Co., 1963.

Calderón de la Barca, Francis Erksine. (English) (1812-1882), *Life in Mexico*. New York: Dutton, 1931.

Campos, Ruben M. *Chapultepec, Its Legend and its History*. Translated by Luis Bozzo Jr. Mexico: 1922.

Cante, Pablo C. de. *Architectura Mexicana del Siglo XVI*. Editorial Porrua, Mexico, 1954.

Caso, Alfonso. *The Aztecs, People of the Sun*. Translated by Lowell Dunhan, Norman: University of Oklahoma Press, 1957.

Cervantes de Salazar, Fransisco. *Life in the Imperial and Loyal City of Mexico in New Spain and the Pontifical University of Mexico as described in the Dialogues for the study of the Latin Language*. (1554). Published in Facsimile. Translated by Minnie Lee Barrett Shepard, Introduction and notes by Carlos Eduardo Castaneda, Austin: University of Texas Press, 1953.

————.*México en 1554 y Túmulo Imperial*. Edited by Edmundo O'Gorman, México: Editorial Porrua, S.A., 1961.

Cetto, Max. *Modern Architecture in Mexico*. New York: Praeger, 1961.

Chavero, Alfredo. *Los azteca o mexica, Fundación de la Ciudad de México-Tenochtitlán*. México: Biblioteca Minima, 1955.

Clavijero, Francisco Javier. *Historia Antigua de México*. México: 1945.

Cortés, Hernán. *Dispatches from Mexico to Charles V*. edited by A. Grove Day, New York: American Book Co., 1935.

Díaz del Castillo, Bernal. *The Discovery and Conquest of Mexico 1517-1521*. Edited by Genaro García, translated by A.P. Maudslay, Introduction to the American edition by Irving A. Leonard; New York: Farrar, Strauss & Cudahy, 1956.

Downing, Todd. *The Mexican Earth*. New York: Doubleday, Doran & Co., 1940.

El Conquistador Anónimo (Alonso de Ulua?). *Relación de algunas cosas de la Nueva España y de la gran Ciudad de Temestitlan México*, escrita por un compañero de Hernán Cortés (c. 1535), México: Editorial America, 1941.

Flores Guerrero, Raul. *Las Capillas Posas de México*. México: Ediciones de Arte, Colección Anahuac, 1948.

Galindo y Villa, Jesús. *Historia Sumaria de la Ciudad de México*. México: Editorial Cultura, 1925.

Gante, Pablo C de. *Architectura Mexicana del Siglo XVI*. Editorial Porrua, Mexico, 1954.

Garay, Fransisco de. *El Valle de México, Apuntes sobre su hidrographia*. In Maudslay's notes in *The Discovery and Conquest of Mexico*, Diaz: 1956.

Gil Alcocer, Hector. *Análisis del Aspecto Urbano de la Ciudad de México-Tenochtitlán*. México: 1951.

Gonzales Obregón, Luis. *México Viejo*. México: Editorial Patria, 1959.

Guerrero Moctezuma, Francisco. *Las Plazas en las ciudades de la Nueva España en relación con las ordenanzas en nuevas poblaciones de Felipe II*. Mexico: 1934.

Hardoy, Jorge. *Urban Planning in Pre-Columbian America*. Edited by George R. Collins. New York: George Braziller, 1968.

Información de méritos y servicios de Alonso García Bravo, alarife que trazó la Ciudad de México (1604). Edited by J.I. Mantecón, forward by Manuel Toussaint. México: Universidad, 1956.

Kilbam, Walter H. *Mexican Architecture of the Vice-Regal Period*. New York: Longmans, Greene & Co., 1927.

Kubler, George. *Mexican Architecture of the Sixteenth Century*. New Haven, Conn. (Yale), 1948. 2 vols.

Marquina, Ignacio. *Templo Mayor de México*, I.N.A.H. Mexico, 1957.

McAndrew, John. *The Open-Air Churches of Sixteenth Century México*. Cambridge, Mass.: Harvard University Press, 1965.

Mumford, Lewis. *The Culture of Cities*. New York: Harcourt, Brace & Co., 1938.

Novo, Salvador. *Nueva Grandeza Mexicana; Ensayo sobre la Ciudad de México y sus Alrededores en 1946*. México: Editorial Hermes, 1946.

Prescott, William Hickley. *The Conquest of Mexico*. New York: Heritage Press, 1949.

Reps, John W. *The Making of Urban America*. Princeton, N.J.: Princeton University Press, 1965.

Sahagún, Fray Bernardino de. *Historia General de las cosas de la Nueva España*. México: 1938.

Sanford, Trent Elwood. *The Story of Architecture in Mexico*. New York: W.W. Norton & Co., 1947.

Smith, Clive Bamford. *Builders in the Sun*, with foreword by
Dr. Jose Villagrán García; New York: Architectural
Publishing Co., 1967.

Teja Zabre, Alfonso. *Chapultepec*. México: 1938.

Toussaint, Manual. *Paseos Coloniales*. Introduction by Justino
Fernandez, edited by Xavier Moyssin Echeverría;
México: Imprenta Universitaria, 1962.

Vargas Martínez, Ubaldo. *La Ciudad de México 1325-1960*.
México: 1961.

Villiers-Stuart, C.M. *Spanish Gardens*. London: B.T. Batsford,
Ltd., 1929.

ARTICLES

"La Ciudad de México No. VI: Sus Casas," *Artes de México*, No. 97-98
XIV (1967).

"La Ciudad de México No. IV: Sus Plazas," *Artes de México*, No. 109,
XV (1968).

"La Ciudad de México No. VI: Sus Plazas," *Artes de México*, No. 110,
XV (1968).

"Los Jardines de Nuestra Ciudad," *Comercio*, X-100m (Feb. 1, 1969),
pp. 16-22.

Mayorga, Mauricio Gómez. "Parques y Jardines en la Ciudad de México,"
Comercio, X-100, (Feb. 1, 1969) pp.8-9.

———. "La Architectura Contemporanea en México," *Artes de México*,
IX-36, (Oct., 1961).

Museo Nacional de Historia, "Castillo de Chapultepec," *I.N.A.H.* México,
1964.

Nuttall, Zelia. "The gardens of ancient Mexico," in *Smithsonian Institution
Annual Report 1923*, Washington, 1925.

Stanislawski, Dan. "Early Spanish Town Planning in the New World."
The Geographical Review, Vol. 37., p. 103, 1947.

INDEX